Into the painting . . .

"What do you think?" Steve asked Uncle Fong. When he sat back, the sunlight from the window flooded the room. His grandfather and uncle crowded around.

"But what will you do when we want to go to bed?" Uncle Fong asked.

Quickly Steve painted a shutter. "We'll cover up the window with this."

"It looks just like home," Uncle Fong murmured as he gazed at the village.

Grandfather squinted at the window. "The trees look like they're swaying in a breeze," he said. "That's very artful of you, Steve."

Uncle Fong rested against the window as he sniffed the air. "And the peaches are just ripening. You got the season just right, boy."

As Uncle Fong bent to touch a peach, he leaned too far. With a cry, he toppled straight into the painting.

ALSO BY LAURENCE YEP

The Dragon Prince
Dream Soul
The Imp That Ate My Homework
The Rainbow People
The Star Fisher
Sweetwater
Tongues of Jade

GOLDEN MOUNTAIN CHRONICLES

The Serpent's Children
Mountain Light
Dragon's Gate
A Newbery Honor Book
The Traitor
Dragonwings
A Newbery Honor Book
The Red Warrior
Coming Soon
Child of the Owl
Sea Glass
Thief of Hearts

CHINATOWN MYSTERIES

The Case of the Goblin Pearls
Chinatown Mystery #1
The Case of the Lion Dance
Chinatown Mystery #2
The Case of the Firecrackers
Chinatown Mystery #3

DRAGON OF THE LOST SEA FANTASIES

Dragon of the Lost Sea
Dragon Steel
Dragon Cauldron
Dragon War

EDITED BY LAURENCE YEP

American Dragons
Twenty-Five Asian American Voices

LAURENCE YEP

THE MAGIC PAINTBRUSH

DRAWINGS BY SULING WANG

HarperTrophy®
An Imprint of HarperCollinsPublishers

To Felicia, who has a magical brush of her own
—L.Y.

Harper Trophy® is a registered trademark of HarperCollins Publishers Inc.

The Magic Paintbrush
Text copyright © 2000 by Laurence Yep
Illustrations copyright © 2000 by Suling Wang

Library of Congress Cataloging-in-Publication Data
Yep, Laurence.
The magic paintbrush / by Laurence Yep ; drawings by Suling Wang.
p. cm.
Summary: A magic paintbrush transports Steve and his elderly caretakers from their drab apartment in Chinatown to a world of adventures.
ISBN 0-06-028199-5. — ISBN 0-06-028200-2 (lib. bdg.)
ISBN 0-06-440852-3 (pbk.)
1. Chinese Americans—Juvenile fiction. [1. Chinese Americans—Fiction. 2. Grandfathers—Fiction. 3. Old age—Fiction. 4. Magic—Fiction. 5. Wishes—Fiction. 6. Orphans—Fiction. 7. Chinatown (San Francisco, Calif.)—Fiction.] I. Wang, Suling, ill. II. Title.
PZ7.Y44Mag 2000   99-34959
[Fic]—dc21   CIP

Typography by Carla Weise
❖
First Harper Trophy edition, 2003

Visit us on the World Wide Web!
www.harperchildrens.com

CONTENTS

Failure

Steve sat in the school yard long after school was over. He was really scared. What would his grandfather say when Steve went home? He preferred shivering outside to facing his grandfather.

All around the school yard the buildings of Chinatown crowded shoulder to shoulder. Everything here seemed so strange. It was one big nightmare.

Resting his head on his knees, he closed his eyes. Maybe when he opened them, he'd be back home where there were regular houses and real lawns. And his mother and father would be waiting in the doorway.

He tried to remember what they looked like, but all he could see were flames. He screwed his eyebrows together as he fought to recall them. No matter how hard he struggled, they were always hidden by fire.

He was all alone now—except for his grandfather. And that was the same thing as being alone.

Grandfather was mean. Steve knew his grandfather didn't want him. After the fire he had to go live in Chinatown. Grandfather had told Steve he could bring only one box with him to Chinatown. How do you put your whole life into just one box? Not that he had much left after the fire. He had lost everything . . . his parents, his toys, his books, his clothes.

And everything Steve did just made his grandfather meaner. He never spoke to Steve except to scold him. And now Steve was sure his grandfather was going to blow his top.

Steve had always tried to get good grades when his parents were alive, especially in art, his favorite class. His parents had hung his best paintings in their offices so their coworkers could admire them. The rest of their house had been decorated with them.

All that was gone in one terrible, fiery night.

Now, because his grandfather was poor, there was never money for watercolors or paper. Steve had to make everything last: his clothes, his paper, his pens, and especially his paints and paintbrush.

Back at home, he would have enjoyed today's assignment. He would have painted a great portrait of the new president, Kennedy.

However, today at school the brush had worn out.

The tired hairs had refused to keep their point and had split into three parts.

His third-grade teacher had criticized his painting. "You're straining my eyes. I feel like I'm seeing triple. How many times have I reminded you to get a new brush?"

"I'm sorry," Steve said. He was too ashamed to tell her that he could not afford a new one.

"You should have obeyed me. Maybe this will teach you," she had said, and she wrote a big "F" on his picture.

The rest of the day Steve was in a daze. He had never gotten an F before, and he had never thought he would get it in his best subject.

He opened his eyes now. He was still caught in the nightmare, and it was getting worse. The Chinatown shadows were growing longer. All around him the doorways started to look like mouths. They stretched wide to swallow him.

Finally he got more scared of the Chinatown streets than of his grandfather. Slowly he walked through the narrow alleys until he reached his grandfather's apartment building. Steve couldn't think of the ugly building as his home.

The tenement house was all of dark-red brick. Dirt made the bricks look even darker. It had a narrow front that rose for three stories.

As Steve mounted the steps, he heard shouting from the back. Everyone in the tenement shared the kitchen, with its sink and stove. The tenants were supposed to take turns, but there were always fights.

"Hey," Mrs. Lee yelled, "it's time to get out of here."

"I can't help it," Mrs. Chin shouted back. "The people ahead of me took longer."

"And afterward clean up the stove and the sink for the next person," Mrs. Lee snapped.

Their angry voices chased him up the dim stairs. Their words nipped at his ears. The Chins and the Lees always seemed to be fighting over something.

He stopped when he reached his floor. The landlord, Mr. Pang, never replaced the ceiling lights. The hallway stretched on like a black tunnel. It looked like raw, dark dough that someone was pulling longer and longer.

There was just one toilet on each floor of the tenement. It was always leaking. Steve could hear it dripping now. And yet Mr. Pang was always raising the rent. Whenever anyone complained, Mr. Pang told them to go back to China if they didn't like his building.

Steve found his way by smell: past Mrs. Soo, who was burning incense in her room. He found his way by ear: past Mr. Jow and his bad, bloody cough. He found his way by touch: past the old, moldy mattress leaning against the wall.

Groping, he found the door to the room he shared with his grandfather and Uncle Fong. Taking a deep breath, he twisted the doorknob and stepped inside.

The bare bulb dangling from the ceiling cast a harsh light over the tiny, cramped room. The paint on the old walls was peeling or stained orange and brown where the rain had leaked or pipes had burst. It was tiny compared to his old bedroom. This room was barely ten by ten feet. A small table stood near the doorway as he entered. On the table were their hot plate, glasses, dishes, and chopsticks. None of the dishes matched. Most of them came from restaurants where Grandfather had washed dishes.

Against one wall was the bed that belonged to Uncle Fong. On the opposite wall was Steve and Grandfather's bed. The room was a crazy quilt of colors. Every inch was crammed with boxes and shopping bags full of Grandfather's and Uncle Fong's stuff. The room was so packed, there was barely enough room for Steve's things.

His grandfather looked at him angrily.

"Where have you been?" Grandfather frowned. "We've waited to have dinner with you."

That made Steve feel more guilty. He knew that Grandfather and Uncle Fong had been working since dawn that morning.

Uncle Fong was sitting on his bed, soaking his feet in a basin of water. "Shame on you," he scolded. "Eight-year-old boys shouldn't be out this late on their own."

Uncle Fong was not a blood relation. He came from Dragon Back, a village in China next to Grandfather's, and they had been friends since they were boys. After Grandmother had died, they had become roommates. They had lived together for a long time now.

Grandfather glared at Steve. "Native-born have no brains."

"Your grandfather was worried sick," Uncle Fong said. "Don't you realize how hard it is for a man your grandfather's age to have to raise a boy?"

"You were worried about me?" Steve asked, surprised. He had thought his grandfather would be glad if he left.

"Of course," his grandfather snapped. Annoyed, he plugged in the hot plate and turned it on.

Mr. Pang did not allow hot plates. However, it was easier to cook meals in their room than in the kitchen. Soon Steve could smell the sausages and vegetables heating up on top of the rice in the pot.

His stomach started to growl. It had been hours since lunchtime.

"Where were you, you bad boy?" Uncle Fong demanded.

How could he tell Grandfather and Uncle Fong about what had happened at school? Too miserable to speak, Steve sat upon the bed.

Grandfather came over and felt his forehead. "What's wrong, boy? Are you sick?"

Steve knew he could not put it off any longer, so he reached into his backpack and took out his picture. "I tried my best, but the teacher gave me an F."

He tensed, getting ready for the scolding. Would his grandfather get so mad, he'd throw Steve out?

Then what would Steve do?

Grandfather's Suitcase

Grandfather studied the picture for a while. He squinted at it up close and then held it far away. Finally he harrumphed. "Actually, I think it's rather clever. How did you copy everything three times the same way? It's very, very artful. I would have given you an A."

Uncle Fong came over on his wet feet to look at it himself. "Fool, he didn't do that deliberately. There's something wrong with his brush."

"Let me see your paintbrush," Grandfather said, holding out his hand.

Steve got out his precious watercolors and opened the lid. "I've tried to make it last." He held up the tired brush.

"It's got less hair than Fong." Grandfather rubbed

the top of Uncle Fong's bald head.

Uncle Fong straightened up. "Those cheap brushes never last long. You've got to buy him a new one."

Grandfather patted his pants pockets, but they were empty. "I don't get paid until Friday."

Uncle Fong went back to his bed and set his feet in the basin. "I'm broke too," he said.

"Then it's more Fs until next week." Steve sniffed. Tears started to roll down his cheeks.

His grandfather hesitated and then patted him clumsily on the shoulder. "Don't cry. It's not your fault. It's not anyone's fault."

That only made Steve feel worse, and he cried even harder.

"Well, well," his grandfather said, scratching his cheek and studying him. Suddenly he squatted down. When Steve had tried that position once, he had had to give up. His hip and leg joints had ached too much.

Reaching beneath the bed, Grandfather dragged out an old brown suitcase. "I got all this old junk I should have thrown away a long time ago."

Curious, Steve wiped his eyes on his sleeve. "Are there any pictures of my parents in there?" He had lost all his photographs in the fire.

Grandfather became solemn. His eyes narrowed and his lips pressed together tightly. He looked as if Steve had kicked him. That always happened whenever Steve mentioned his parents. His grandfather must hate Steve's parents as much as he hated Steve.

"What's past is past," Grandfather scolded. "You can't spend the rest of your life missing someone or something. Life is hard, so you have to be hard too. You've got a lot to learn about being a Chinatowner. Chinatowners have to grow up fast. Uncle Fong did. I did. Now it's your turn."

Steve had never felt more lonely. Grandfather could be really strange. Steve would never understand him.

"I'm sorry," Steve said quickly, before Grandfather could lose his temper again.

Grandfather looked back at the suitcase. "Anyway, this junk is even older than your father."

The brass locks clicked up, and Grandfather lifted the top. The smell of sandalwood filled the room. It was pungent but pleasant. Steve leaned to look over Grandfather's shoulder. There were many objects inside. He pointed toward a metal tonguelike object. "What's that, Grandfather?"

"A shoehorn." Grandfather picked it up and placed it near his heel. "It helps you put on your shoes." He held it up so Steve could read what was printed on the shoehorn. "It's from the old Roos Brothers Department Store." He put the shoehorn back into the suitcase. "I got my first pair of American shoes there. I thought they were so fancy. And then afterward I had my first ice cream. It was at Blum's."

"I don't suppose you have a souvenir from that?"

Uncle Fong asked, and smacked his lips. "It looks like you've got everything else in there."

"Fifty years of junk," Grandfather agreed.

His words made it sound as if he didn't care, but he was looking inside the suitcase wistfully. Steve would have liked to ask Grandfather more questions. Were there reminders of Grandmother in there? But he was too scared to ask.

All the attention had made his grandfather cranky. Shifting the suitcase, he shielded the contents with his body. "It's all from places no one cares about anymore," he mumbled. "When I got some time, I'm going to throw it all out."

Steve had felt terrible when he had lost everything in the fire. "No, don't do that. All those things must have special memories, or you wouldn't have kept them."

"Don't encourage him. He's a regular pack rat," Uncle Fong said.

"At least I've got memories. What have you got?" Grandfather asked Uncle Fong.

Now that water had softened his corns and calluses, Uncle Fong began to trim them. "Nothing. I should have stayed in Dragon Back. I can't even stay warm here. No heat in the meat-packing place and no heat here. But it was always hot back home."

"I wish you'd stop talking about China all the time," Grandfather grumbled. "I'd settle for a room with a window. It'd be nice to see a little blue sky once in a while. All I see the whole day is dirty plates. Some-times what I see on them makes my stomach get sick. Then I don't want to eat."

"At least you get variety. When you cut chickens all day, all you see is one chicken rump after another." Uncle Fong made a face. "I see chicken rumps even in my dreams now."

Grandfather sighed to Steve. "Can you believe any-one trusts that sour old man with a knife?"

Steve did not answer. He didn't want the teasing to escalate into another one of their arguments. They could be like two boys in a school yard. The playful insults could go on until one of them went over a line. Then words could turn to punches.

As Grandfather continued to sift through the contents of the suitcase, Steve heard mysterious clink-ings and clackings. They sounded like music, and Grandfather looked as if he were far away. Steve won-dered what Grandfather was remembering.

"Ah," Grandfather finally said when he found what he wanted. "Here. You can use this, Steve."

When he turned around, Grandfather had a brush in his hands.

The Magic Paintbrush

The paintbrush was a work of art in itself. Its bamboo stem had been intricately carved. Though Steve studied the carvings, he could not make them out. They were too old and worn.

And yet the brush itself seemed new. Its blue hairs looked pure and crisp. They tapered to a sharp point.

Grandfather twirled the stem between his fingers. "My grandfather made this for me before I came here. He said the hairs came from a unicorn's tail. Or was it a dragon's beard? Here, boy. Take the brush."

Though Steve longed to touch it, he kept his hands at his sides. "I couldn't use this. It's too special."

"Go on, boy," Uncle Fong urged. "That was only a story his grandfather told him. Dragons and unicorns. Bah! I bet there was some poor horse back in China that felt a draft on its south end."

"This looks new," Steve said. "Didn't you ever use it?"

"I was supposed to continue my art lessons here, but I was always too busy working." Grandfather thrust the brush at Steve. "Go on. It's just gathering dust."

"Thank you." Breathlessly, Steve took the paintbrush. He remembered to add, "Granddad."

"Forget it," his grandfather said, but he sounded pleased.

The bamboo stem felt warm in Steve's fingers. It began to tingle. The carvings even seemed to wriggle, tickling his fingers. The paintbrush begged to be used. He couldn't wait any longer. "Can I try it out?"

"So you like that old thing?" his grandfather asked shyly.

"Eat your dinner first," Uncle Fong scolded.

Steve's stomach was growling again, but he wanted to paint even more. "I'm not hungry," he fibbed.

Grandfather studied him thoughtfully. "You love to paint, don't you?"

Steve caressed the stem. "It's my favorite subject in school."

Grandfather smiled. "I used to be just like you. Well, go on. We'll get things ready."

"You spoil him," Uncle Fong grumbled.

"I don't want him turning out all sour like you," Grandfather teased.

"You're a fine one to talk. You'd outsour a lemon,"

Uncle Fong said. He watched Steve sit eagerly on the floor. Scratching his nose, Uncle Fong pulled out a pile of paper from under his bed. "I went through the trash can in the office. I figure you can use the backs." He tried to look like he didn't care. "Or you can just toss the paper in the trash."

"Thank you, Uncle Fong," Steve said. Finding paper was always a problem. Fortunately there was an office at the meat plant. "Can I throw away your basin of water?"

"If you like," Uncle Fong said, trying hard not to smile.

Steve went to the bathroom and emptied the basin into the sink. After he had cleaned it out, he put in some fresh water and returned to the room. He had left the door open so that he could find his way back in the dark hallway.

As Steve returned, he could hear Grandfather and Uncle Fong talking.

"I want a steak tonight," Uncle Fong demanded. Every night he asked for something expensive. It was his idea of a joke.

"Beef costs too much," Grandfather snapped. Then his face took on a mischievous look. "However," he added, "tonight we have some for you."

"Really?" Uncle Fong said, surprised.

"Of course we do," Grandfather said. "Would I lie?" He did not give Uncle Fong a chance to reply.

"You remember Ah Deer, the butcher? He owed me money from a bet. So he paid me off. I . . . uh . . . snuck it into the pot when you weren't looking. The beef is almost as tender as Dragon Back beef."

"That steak would have to be very tender then. Is it?" Uncle Fong asked Grandfather.

As soon as Steve appeared in the doorway, Grandfather crooked a finger at him. When Steve leaned over, Grandfather whispered, "Let's grant Uncle's wish. Can you paint him a steak?"

Since Uncle Fong had given him the paper, Steve didn't know if he should help with the prank. "I don't know . . ." he said uncertainly.

Grandfather just winked. "Come on, boy. Be a sport."

Grandfather had never asked him to share anything, even a joke. So Steve got his paints and selected a sheet of white paper. On the front was a list of prices, but the back was pure white. When Steve picked up the brush, he felt the tingle again.

Steve painted a steak bone. The brush tip darted hungrily at the paper like a snake. He put in the red meat and the white veins and even remembered the government seal of approval.

Just as he finished, the lid began to bounce up and down on the pot.

"Dinner's ready," Grandfather announced, and lifted the lid.

Uncle Fong got up from his bed and went over to the pot. "I thought you said there was beef," he complained.

"No, no, there's a steak all for you." Grandfather waved at Steve to give the painting to Uncle Fong.

When Steve grasped the painting, it tingled against his fingertips. He felt as if he had rubbed his shoes fast over a carpet. And the tingling spread through his whole hand.

Dangling from his hand was a big, juicy, red steak. "What's going on?" he asked, scared.

Grandfather and Uncle Fong had their backs to him. When he turned around, Grandfather gave a jump. "Where did that come from?"

"It just appeared," Steve said as he turned the steak this way and that. He studied it from several angles. "I . . . I just painted it," Steve said.

Still holding the lid, Grandfather inspected it.

Uncle Fong leaned over and gave it a sniff. "It smells like beef."

Grandfather poked it with a finger. "It feels like beef."

Uncle Fong folded his arms. "Ha, ha. Very funny, Steve. You're an even worse prankster than your grandfather. You can't fool me. That steak came from Ah Deer."

"No. I was kidding about Ah Deer. The brush really is magic," Grandfather said, staring at it.

Uncle Fong got a frying pan from beneath the table. "Well, magic or not, we're going to eat it." He began to rummage around. "Let's see. Where's the knife?"

Steve picked up the brush. It felt warm, as if it were alive. "Maybe I can make one. What kind would you like?"

Uncle Fong still thought Steve was playing a joke. "I don't care as long as it has an edge."

Quickly, Steve cleaned his brush. Selecting another piece of paper, he began to paint a cleaver with a sharp edge. Once again the brush almost seemed to pull his fingers along. When he was finished, he put the brush down. Then he picked up the paper.

He felt a tingle pass through the paper and into his hand. Carefully he laid the picture down on his bed. Suddenly a cleaver appeared on top of the covers.

Uncle Fong set the pan down with a clunk. "Huh! The brush really is magic."

Heart's Desire

"We're rich! We're rich! We're rich!" Uncle Fong shouted, and did a little dance. He stopped when the neighbors beneath them pounded on the ceiling.

Uncle Fong was too happy to stop completely. "We're rich, we're rich," he whispered back to the neighbors.

Sitting back down on his bed, he said in an even lower voice, "Now Steve can paint money whenever we need it."

Grandfather poked him in the chest. "Fool! Everyone in Chinatown knows we're poor. They'll think we stole it from someone."

"Steve could demonstrate for them," Uncle Fong said. "Then he can paint me a big, fancy car." He raised his hands and pretended to turn a big steering wheel.

Grandfather lowered Uncle Fong's arms. "Someone will steal the brush then," Grandfather said. "If people knew our secret, they would want things too. They could gang up on us."

Uncle Fong looked very frustrated. He began to slice the beef quickly. "If you can't use it, what good is magic then?"

Grandfather rubbed his chin. "We can use the brush. We just have to be careful. We must continue to dress the same. We must act the same. We must follow the same routine."

Uncle Fong groaned. "You mean go to work?"

"And school," Grandfather said, glancing at Steve.

"And tell our secret to no one." Uncle Fong started to fry the beef with quick flicks of his wooden chopsticks. "Well, at least we can feast every night."

"We don't know how much magic is in the brush," Grandfather said. "Magic isn't like ink. It doesn't work like a disposable pen." He spread his arms. "If we don't use it correctly, we're out of luck and out of magic. We need to use the paintbrush carefully."

Uncle Fong looked toward Heaven. "Isn't that just my luck? Now I can't even count on eating well."

Grandfather crossed his legs. "What would you do if you were rich?"

Uncle Fong sulked. "I told you. I'd drive a big car."

"That's a toy." Grandfather clasped his hands over his knees. "You'd get bored with it soon. And wait till you try to find a parking space."

"Chinatown is jammed with cars and trucks day and night," Uncle Fong admitted.

Grandfather cleared his throat. "In other words, what would make you happy?"

"Well, I . . ." Uncle Fong said, and then scratched his head. "You know, I'm not sure. I never thought about that part."

Grandfather wagged one leg up and down. "Just so. None of us have. We don't want money. We want what money can buy. We want our hearts' desire, as the poets say."

Steve looked at his grandfather, impressed. He hadn't thought Grandfather was such a wise man.

Grandfather awkwardly patted Steve on the back. "Steve can give us our dreams."

Uncle Fong shook his head. "I gave up dreaming a long time ago."

"Then start again, old man," Grandfather said.

The beef sizzled in the pan. "In the meantime, can we eat?" Steve asked. He had not tasted beef in a long time.

"This boy is as smart as his grandfather. The beef's done." Uncle Fong laughed and ladled the beef into a dish.

All through dinner everyone kept looking at the magic brush. Finally Uncle Fong set down his bowl and patted his stomach. "What a feast."

"Almost as good as Dragon Back beef?" Grandfather asked.

Uncle Fong was feeling good. For once something had equaled his old home. "Almost."

When they had cleaned up everything, they sat down on their beds. As Steve picked up the brush again in his right hand, he felt it tremble in his fingers. "So what do I paint next?"

"I would like a peach from home." Uncle Fong closed his eyes. "One with a lovely scent that fills the room. And when you bite into it, the juice runs into your mouth. And it's as sweet as summer. And the scent is like perfume."

"That's a tall order," Grandfather said, glancing uncertainly at Steve.

Uncle Fong folded his arms. "That's what I want."

"And anyway, who said you could go first?" Grandfather demanded.

Steve thought he saw a way to please both old men. In his hand he felt the brush twitching eagerly. He had to use two hands to keep it still. "Do you still want a window, Grandfather?"

"Yes," Grandfather said.

"And just when I was starting to think you were smart," Uncle Fong said in disgust. "A window on any of our walls would just look at another brick wall."

Steve turned on his bed and rose to his knees. "No. I think I know what to do."

On the bare wall above his and Grandfather's bed he painted a window that looked just like a Chinese window. He had seen one in an antique store. The window frame was of carved wood that had been painted red. It was covered with flowers and dragons and unicorns.

Steve's window turned out perfectly. Feeling much more confident now, he turned to Uncle Fong. "What was your home like?"

Uncle Fong licked his lips. "Well, Dragon Back village sat on the side of a valley. There were pine trees along the ridge. And there were rice fields on the valley floor. They looked just like emerald patches." As he talked, the frown lines left the corners of his mouth. He looked younger as he remembered his hometown. "And the orchards surrounded the village. You could always find my family's pet duck there. It was always hunting for food."

As Uncle Fong stood over his shoulder, Steve began to paint the village between the window frames. He hardly needed Uncle Fong's coaching. The brush already seemed to know exactly what to paint. The ridge rising from the valley was shaped like a dragon. The green-tiled roofs were like scales. The pine trees stood up like spikes from the dragon's spine. The fields on the valley floor looked like stained glass.

Finally Steve painted an orchard of peach trees just for Uncle Fong. The peaches shimmered like pale stars. As a last touch he added a duck under the trees.

"What do you think?" Steve asked Uncle Fong. When he sat back, the sunlight from the window flooded the room. His grandfather and uncle crowded around.

"Does it still feel like a tomb in here now?" Steve asked Grandfather timidly.

He was pleased when Grandfather shook his head. "Blue sky—just like I always wanted."

"But what will you do when we want to go to bed?" Uncle Fong asked.

Quickly Steve painted a shutter. "We'll cover up the window with this."

"It looks just like home," Uncle Fong murmured as he gazed at the village.

Grandfather squinted at the window. "The trees look like they're swaying in a breeze," he said. "That's very artful of you, Steve."

Uncle Fong rested against the window as he sniffed the air. "And the peaches are just ripening. You got the season just right, boy."

As Uncle Fong bent to touch a peach, he leaned too far. With a cry, he toppled straight into the painting.

Home Cooking

"Are you all right?" Steve called.

A tiny Uncle Fong waved to them from inside the picture. "I'm fine. Come on. Join me," he shouted. He sounded far away.

"You old fool! Come back here," Grandfather called urgently.

Uncle Fong made a face at Grandfather. "I'll race you. Just like the old days."

"I don't have time for your silly games," Grandfather snapped. "What about your corns and calluses?"

"Coward!" Uncle Fong forgot all about his aching feet. He began to run. He looked as excited as a small boy.

When he disappeared among the trees, Grandfather sighed. "We'd better follow him. He might get into trouble. Bring that paintbrush with you, boy." Gingerly,

Grandfather stepped into the window. When he saw it was safe, he let Steve step through the painting.

Together they entered the orchard. Overhead the peaches hung among the leafy green branches. The fruity perfume surrounded them like a cloud.

They heard a rattling sound ahead of them. When they stepped out of the cover of the trees, they saw an odd wooden machine. "What is that?" Steve asked.

"It's a water chain," Grandfather said. "It carries water from the river."

The water chain was a long wooden trough. It led from the river up the slope. Inside the trough was a series of wooden paddles.

Uncle Fong held on to a wooden stick. His feet moved a wheel of wooden pedals. "Come on. I bet I can bring more water up than you."

Grandfather shook his head. "That's how you always tried to trick me into doing that chore."

Uncle Fong tossed his head back and laughed. "It never worked, though." Then he looked at Steve. "When I was your age, boy, I always hated this job. I didn't know how good I had it. This is fun next to working at the meat packer's."

As his feet turned the wheel, the chain moved. Water splashed from the upper end of the trough into a ditch. The ditch fed water into the orchard.

"Ow," said Grandfather. The next moment Steve felt something nip his ankle. He looked at his feet. There squatted a very annoyed and self-important duck.

"I thought it was a pet?" Steve said as he rubbed his leg.

"To be more exact, it was his sister's pet, and she encouraged it to bite boys." Grandfather darted away from the snapping beak.

Uncle Fong jumped down from the pedals. "Go on. Shoo, Coconut." He waved his hands to make it go away.

When the duck charged him, he got down on all fours and began to growl. The duck halted but began to quack angrily. When Uncle Fong barked back, the duck waddled off. Uncle Fong chased it to the edge of the orchard. Then he stood up.

"Try a peach, Steve," Uncle Fong said. He plucked three from the nearest branch.

The sweetness soaked into Steve's tongue when he bit into his.

Uncle Fong smacked his lips. "It's just as good as I remembered."

"It's good enough for a banquet in Heaven," Grandfather decided.

They heard a little girl singing. She was a little off-key. Soon she danced into view. In her hand she had a long, red ribbon, which she twirled overhead in circles and spirals.

"That's my big sister, Kitten," Uncle Fong said softly to Steve. "She died many years ago."

"She looks like you," Steve whispered back.

Uncle Fong got annoyed. "No, she's the ugly one. I'm the handsome one," he protested.

"What's the difference? You haven't seen her in years," Grandfather said.

Uncle Fong stared at his sister while she danced. Slowly his mouth worked up into a smile. "Well anyway, Kitten may not have been better-looking than me, but she was always more graceful."

When the ribbon snagged in a tree's branches, Uncle Fong went over to her. "Let me help you, big sister."

When she saw him, her eyes got really big. "Who are you?! Don't you dare steal our fruit!" She began shouting. "Help! Thieves! Rascals!"

Uncle Fong held out his hands to her. "Don't you know me? I've come a long way to see you."

When she frowned, she looked exactly like Uncle Fong. "Well, watch this," Kitten said, and grabbed Uncle Fong's thumb. Then she bit it. Hard.

"Ow!" Uncle Fong said. He wrung his hurt hand in the air.

"That's where her duck gets its personality from." Grandfather laughed.

Uncle Fong clenched his good hand into a fist. "She always had a temper," he explained to Steve.

"It runs in the family," Grandfather said.

"What do you mean? I'm the sweet, cheerful one in the family," Uncle Fong said indignantly.

Kitten ran off, calling out, "Help, help, thieves, robbers, bandits!"

Steve grabbed Uncle Fong's wrist. "We'd better leave, or we'll get into real trouble."

They heard a gong sound somewhere among the trees. A man started to shout, "Alarm, alarm!"

"There'll be a mob coming soon," Grandfather said.

"But it's my clan," Uncle Fong protested.

"They won't know you. You've grown old," Grandfather warned.

Steve tugged at Uncle Fong. "They'll just beat you."

Uncle Fong sighed and then turned in a slow circle, looking at everything. "I want to remember it just as it is," he murmured.

Suddenly an object whistled by his ear.

Men, women, and children came out from the trees. They held sticks and brooms and hoes. They waved them over their heads menacingly.

Kitten led them. Her duck waddled angrily at her heels.

In one hand she held a basket. "Thieves, robbers!" she shouted angrily. Then she took something from the basket and threw it.

"Ow." Uncle Fong jumped when it hit him.

The missile rolled near Steve's feet. He picked it up. "It looks like a meat dumpling, but it feels like a rock."

Kitten pelted Uncle Fong with more dumplings.

Finally Uncle Fong turned and raced past them. "It must be one of her cooking mistakes. She was the worst cook in four districts."

Grandfather yelled to Steve, "Run, boy. She's got enough dumplings to knock out an elephant."

The Radio

Ahead of them, they saw, Grandfather's window hung in the air.

"I'll help you through the window," Steve said. He made a cup with his hands.

"No, you first, boy!" Picking Steve up by the waist, Grandfather threw him through the window onto the bed.

As Steve bounced off the mattress, Grandfather tumbled after him. Uncle Fong was the last one through.

With a groan Uncle Fong rolled off the bed and stood up. "So much for sentiment," he grumbled.

Grandfather complained as he got up finally. "My bruises have bruises. They should have named her Tiger, not Kitten."

"Stupid paintbrush," Uncle Fong said as he sat on his bed. He looked ready to cry.

"Here's a souvenir from Dragon Back." Grandfather held up a peach pit between his index finger and thumb. Getting down on his knees, he felt underneath his bed until he came up with a small tin. Then he deposited the peach pit safely in the tin and gave it to Uncle Fong. "Plant this someday and have your own peaches."

Uncle Fong cradled the tin. "Thank you, friend."

Grandfather nudged Steve. "It's your turn to make a wish."

Steve had been thinking about this. He had been growing excited since the idea had first come to him. His heart was pounding now. "I'd like to see my parents again."

Grandfather looked as if he were suddenly in pain. "They've passed on, boy."

Normally Steve would not have risked making Grandfather angry, but the brush had given him new courage. "So had Uncle Fong's sister Kitten. But we saw her. Don't you miss them?"

Grandfather squirmed uncomfortably. "Of course. But you've seen how quirky the paintbrush is. Who knows what will happen?"

Steve couldn't bear to give up now. "But I already have so much trouble remembering them. I try and I try, but I can't see their faces. It's like . . . it's like losing them all over again."

Grandfather looked thoughtful. Then he said softly, "True."

"Then how are you going to paint them?" asked Uncle Fong.

Getting on his knees, Grandfather slid his suitcase out from under the bed again. Steve sniffed the wonderful, mysterious scents as Grandfather opened the lid. Grandfather rummaged around for a little bit. Then he took out a small packet. It was wrapped in red silk.

Reverently he removed the wrapping and held up a black-and-white photo. It seemed to be of someone's living room. On a table sat a big, old-fashioned radio. In front of it a man and woman stood together. The man was in a tuxedo, and the woman was in a fluffy gown. They were holding hands as if they were about to dance. They were so young, they didn't look like his parents.

Steve studied it carefully, trying to memorize their faces. Then he began to paint on a sheet of paper.

Grandfather swallowed. "I shouldn't let you do this. You're just building up your hopes for nothing. And you're going to feel even more hurt than before." However, Grandfather just sat and watched.

So Steve went on painting. He worked quickly, afraid his grandfather would stop him. Many times he looked at the photograph. His hand almost shook with excitement. He concentrated as hard as he could. He wanted to make the magic happen.

When he was done, he put the brush down and studied his work.

"It looks just like them," Grandfather said.

"Do you really think so?" Steve said.

Grandfather studied Steve's eager face. He nodded.

But this time there was no tingle to the picture. Steve rubbed his fingers back and forth over the paper. There still was no spark.

"It didn't work," he said sadly.

"See? There's only so much the paintbrush can do." Grandfather sighed.

Between his fingers Steve felt the paintbrush expand and contract. He thought it was trying to say it was sorry. "It has a personality like a real person," he said.

"A very funny person," Uncle Fong grunted. "One who likes to play mean tricks."

"You were right," Steve said to his grandfather. He wrapped his arms around himself and rocked back and forth. "It's bad to hope, because it just hurts when you fail."

Tears stung the corners of his eyes. He swiped them with the back of his hand.

"Next time listen to me," Grandfather said. He wiped at his eyes. "Must have gotten something in my eyes," he muttered. However, Steve thought Grandfather must have been feeling just as bad as he did.

He stared. "You don't hate my parents?"

Grandfather kept wiping at his eyes. "What made you think that?"

Steve was afraid that he had gone too far. "Because you always get so mad when I talk about them," he said, frightened.

Grandfather gave a snuffle. "What do you expect? If you kick me, of course I'm going to lose my temper. It's the same thing when you try to make me recall them. Why do you keep doing that all the time? Doesn't it hurt you, too?"

"Sure," Steve said, "but as long as I remember them, they're still alive in a way."

Grandfather was silent for a while before he finally scratched his cheek. "I never thought about it that way."

Uncle Fong jerked his head at Grandfather. "You and me, we're two tough old clams who don't like to talk about things. But the boy grew up different."

Grandfather drew his eyebrows together as he studied Steve. Finally he took a deep breath and let it out. "I guess you did. So you have to mourn in your own way. All right. When you need to, ask me about them."

Now that Steve had permission, he suddenly felt very shy. Instead, he tapped the old radio in the photograph. "What a funny old radio."

"It worked better than any of the new ones," Grandfather said.

"I loved that old radio." Uncle Fong sighed.

"What happened to it?" Steve asked.

Grandfather looked away. "I kept that piece of junk too long."

Uncle Fong frowned at Grandfather. "You owe the boy the truth." He turned to Steve. "Your grandfather sold it to a collector. It paid for your parents' funeral."

Steve felt as if someone had punched him in the stomach. "I'm sorry for being so much trouble."

Grandfather drew himself up proudly. "You do what you have to do for family. So why talk about it?"

Steve thought of how Grandfather had made sure he was first through the window. He'd been wrong. His grandfather really did care. He just didn't talk about it. He showed it by his actions. Somehow Grandfather didn't seem so strange anymore.

Steve touched his grandfather's arm. "Thank you." Steve licked his lips and added, "But there's a lot I still don't understand about Chinatown. Sometimes it would help if you would explain things to me."

His grandfather nodded slowly. "Chinatowners are made, not born."

Satisfied, Steve looked back at the photograph. He touched the handsome young man and the pretty young woman. "They wore those clothes when they danced to rock and roll music?"

"No." Grandfather laughed. "They didn't like the music their friends did. They were ballroom dancers."

"I saw them dance once." Uncle Fong tapped his feet on the floor. "They could have turned professional."

Steve bent over the photo, studying the radio in the background. "What kind of music did they like?"

"American ballroom music, like in the old days," Grandfather said.

"Like when we were young," Uncle Fong said. "Your parents had excellent taste."

Steve squinted harder at the photo. He tried to remember every detail about the radio. Then he began to paint on a sheet of paper. Maybe if he gave it back to his grandfather, he wouldn't feel so sad.

Steve was a little anxious when he had finished. Would the magic work this time? Then he felt the tingle pass through his fingertips. And the radio sat on his bed.

Steve was surprised. "Why did the paintbrush work this time?"

Grandfather rubbed his chin. "Maybe the paintbrush only gives you what it can."

Uncle Fong sighed. "So Dragon Back is gone for good."

"Fool," Grandfather said, tapping his head, "it's still here."

Uncle Fong nodded slowly. "I guess it's better to go back there in my memories than in person."

"You can talk to me about Dragon Back whenever you want," Steve said.

Uncle Fong smiled. "All the good times."

"And we'll do the same with your parents, boy," Grandfather promised. He caressed the radio lightly. "You know, your father used to play this night and day."

Steve plugged it into the outlet by the hot plate and turned it on. A waltz began to play.

"Ah," Grandfather sighed. "That was their favorite tune." He set the photograph where they could see it.

The waltz was as gentle and sweet as a breeze on a hot day. Steve closed his eyes, imagining his father and mother floating across a dance floor.

The next song was a lively number. Grandfather said it was a rumba.

Uncle Fong pointed at the radio. "I remember them dancing to that."

The radio played another half dozen songs. Steve's parents had loved all of them. He set the radio on his lap. He felt the music vibrate in his bones. As he felt his parents' music fill him, he didn't feel so lonely anymore.

Uncle Fong rubbed his chin. "That's funny. There's no commercials on this station." He tried to turn the dial. The station never changed. "And you can only get one station."

Steve hugged the radio. "Can I leave it on tonight? I'll keep it low."

Grandfather looked uncertainly at Uncle Fong. Uncle Fong nodded his head sympathetically.

"It will beat his snoring," Uncle Fong said, jerking a thumb at Grandfather.

They set the radio on the table and turned it low. Then Steve painted some brushes for school. "The magic brush stays home," he said.

They carefully placed it back in Grandfather's

suitcase and got ready for bed. Then Grandfather turned off the room light and lowered the new shutter over the new window. The radio dial still shone in the darkness. It cast a soft glow on the ceiling. As Steve listened to the soft music, he thought he saw shadows of dancers above him. The man and woman whirled round and round as he slowly fell asleep.

The Lady on the Moon

The next night as the radio played softly, Steve asked Grandfather and Uncle Fong, "What shall we do tonight?"

Uncle Fong nodded to the window. "Whatever we decide, you can paint over Dragon Back."

Steve was surprised. "Don't you want to try to go there again sometime?"

Uncle Fong shook his head. "I've been thinking over what the old man said, and he's right. I haven't really lost Dragon Back." He tapped his head. "I've got Dragon Back in here." And he touched his heart. "And in here. That's enough."

"Are you sure?" Grandfather asked gently.

Uncle Fong took a deep breath and then slapped his

knees. "Quite sure. We should be looking forward, not backward."

"But what should I paint?" Steve wondered.

Grandfather rubbed the back of his neck sheepishly. "I've thought and thought about it all day over the soap-suds. But no, you'll just make fun of me."

"It couldn't be any worse than Uncle Fong's," Steve said. "His wish got us chased by a duck."

"It was a very vicious duck," Uncle Fong pointed out.

"Please, Grandfather. We won't laugh," Steve said. "Right?" He looked at Uncle Fong.

Uncle Fong folded his arms. "I guess."

Grandfather clasped his hands upon his lap. "I don't think the paintbrush wants us to go back into the past. So let's try legends. Will you paint me the moon?" He glanced around, waiting for them to tease him.

"Why would you want to go there? There's no life on the moon. The scientists all say so." Uncle Fong began to hop from one leg to the other. "We would need space helmets and space suits."

Steve defended his grandfather. "We'll go wherever Grandfather wants."

Grandfather squeezed Steve's arm gratefully. "I don't want the moon of the newspapers and television. I want to go to the moon the way it's supposed to be. I want Chinatown's moon."

"What moon is that?" Steve asked, puzzled.

"A moon like in the stories they tell in Chinatown," Grandfather explained.

Steve shook his head. "Mom and Dad never told me those stories."

Uncle Fong grunted in disgust. "Kids. They turn their backs on everything."

Grandfather held up a hand. "Easy, Fong." And then he said to Steve, "What Chinese stories did they tell you?"

Steve squirmed. "Well, nothing really." He tried to defend them. "But they were pretty busy."

"Yes, of course." Grandfather placed his hands on his knees while he studied Steve. "Chinatown must seem very strange if you don't know the stories."

Steve wriggled uncomfortably. "Sort of."

"Then we'll make you a Chinatowner," Grandfather said. "First we'll begin with Chinatown's moon." He rose from the bed and shaped a tree with his hands and arms. "Here is the beautiful cassia tree. Its leaves are always green. Its flowers are always in bloom. And its bark is so fragrant—it's cinnamon, you know. The tree can never be cut down. In its shade sits the rabbit. He has a mortar and a pestle to grind things. With them he makes magical pills. Eat one, and you live forever." He described to Steve what a mortar and pestle looked like.

"I always thought it was a mean joke to play on the

Lady on the Moon," Uncle Fong said.

"Who is she?" Steve asked.

"She was the wife of a mighty archer," Grandfather explained. "As a reward for his great feats, Heaven sent him pills of immortality. But his wife swallowed them instead. As punishment Heaven exiled her to the moon."

"Where the rabbit keeps her company," Uncle Fong said. He knocked his hand rhythmically against the wall. "So that's all she hears day and night: the rabbit making pills with a mortar and pestle."

"She would listen from her palace," Grandfather said, and waved a hand. "It would be not too close and not too far from the tree."

As Grandfather described the moon, Steve thought he could almost see it. Excitedly he began to paint over the old picture. Within the window he put the cassia tree and the rabbit and the palace. Its roof slanted steeply, like green-tiled mountains. Creatures stood watch on the roof against fires and lightning and other dangers. A porch led to the main door of the palace, which was perfectly round, like a moon gate.

"Nice," Uncle Fong nodded approvingly. "Just like the old stories."

Steve cleaned his brush. "And what does the Lady on the Moon look like?" Steve asked.

"I always thought she would look a little like your grandmother," Grandfather said.

"I never met her," Steve said.

"And I have no pictures," Grandfather said. "But she was beautiful." And in a deep, pleasant voice, he began to sing about the Lady on the Moon.

Steve went to the radio and snapped it off. He listened to his grandfather for a moment. Finally he began to paint the rabbit's mortar and pestle while his grandfather sang.

Steve had no sooner painted the tools when the rabbit grabbed the pestle and began pounding it into the mortar in time to Grandfather's tune.

Suddenly a silvery light poured from the palace's doorway. The light flooded into their room. Steve felt himself carried along its warm, invisible currents. Still singing, Grandfather looked as if he were floating on a river. Kicking like he was swimming, and waving happily, Uncle Fong was swept into the picture too.

Inside, they landed among giant flowers. They were twice as big as anything on Earth. Some chrysanthemums were as big as cabbages.

Grandfather brushed himself off. "The air's so still here."

"You're lucky there is air," Uncle Fong said.

Grandfather plucked a flower from a bush. "Stop thinking. Just enjoy it."

"Maybe you should ask permission before you pick the flowers," Steve suggested.

"But these all belong to the Lady on the Moon—the most beautiful creature in all the heavens. How dare I speak to her?" Grandfather asked.

Soon he had a handful of flowers. He sniffed them appreciatively. "Ah."

In the distance, over the sound of the pestle pounding in the mortar, they heard another sound. It was a soft hiss-hiss-hiss.

Uncle Fong grabbed Grandfather. "It's a snake. I hate snakes."

Grandfather pushed him away. "There aren't any snakes on the moon."

Suddenly the Lady on the Moon appeared in the doorway. Steve and Grandfather bowed, but Uncle Fong just stood there, staring with his mouth open.

"Mind your manners," Grandfather said, and pinched him.

"Ow." Hastily Uncle Fong lowered his head.

The lady bowed back. Then she moved across the porch toward them. Her long gown trailed behind her, making the hissing noises. The silk whispered as it brushed the wooden floor.

Shading his eyes, Steve asked eagerly, "Does she look like Grandmom?"

When Grandfather smiled, he looked years younger. "Yes."

She smiled sweetly. "I seldom have company."

Grandfather drew himself up. "We seldom go out visiting."

He was just about to present the flowers to her when they heard someone shout, "Hey, who ruined my wall?"

Mighty Mister Pang

"I think you have visitors yourself," the Lady on the Moon said. Whirling around, she disappeared into the palace and slammed the door.

Steve felt as if a giant hand had caught him and pulled him back. The next moment he and his grandfather and Uncle Fong were sitting on the floor of their room.

A small man stood in the middle bouncing up and down on his heels. The cigar dropped from the man's mouth. "How did you step out of the wall?" he demanded.

"We have a magic paintbrush," said Steve. "But who are you? How did you get in here?"

Grandfather shushed Steve. "This is Mr. Pang. He owns this place."

"It's a good thing I showed up today to check on my property." Mr. Pang rubbed his chin. "But what's this about a magic paintbrush?"

"Nothing," Steve said quickly. The landlord looked very sly. He pretended to grow angry as he pointed to the painting. "How dare you wreck my nice clean wall!"

That made Steve mad. "The wall hasn't been painted in years. And what about the burned-out lightbulbs? What about the trash? You should take care of those things first."

Mr. Pang folded his arms sternly. "You vandals can't get away with this outrage. There are laws against this. I'll have all of you arrested and thrown in jail."

"You can't do that to them," Steve said bravely. "I'm the one who painted it."

The landlord rubbed his chin with his big, fat thumb. "Well, I'd be willing to forget what you did if . . ."

Grandfather glared at him. "If what?"

"If you give me the paintbrush," the landlord said.

"Grandfather got this from his grandfather," Steve objected.

"It's yours now, Steve," Grandfather said.

"I'm calling the cops," the landlord threatened. "Where's the phone?"

Steve didn't want to give up the brush, but he loved his grandfather more. "Don't harm my grandfather," he said, and he held out the brush.

Mr. Pang grasped it greedily. "So I just paint something on the wall?"

"Yes," Steve said, "but—"

"I want gold and jade and pearls," Mr. Pang said. He was almost drooling. "No, no, wait. Why stop there? I'll need something to put them in. There are thieves all around." He glanced around and headed for the nearest bare patch of wall.

Steve followed him. "We should warn you—"

"So what do I do? Paint like this?" Mr. Pang began splashing paint crudely on the wall. "I always wanted a house big as the Fairmont Hotel," he said. "With red rugs thick as a pig, and huge chandeliers overhead. Something plush, you know? And classy. And all the plates and cups are real gold. And we never have the same ones twice. Just use them once and throw them away."

Mr. Pang's eyes were big and wide, and he kept chattering excitedly. Hastily he painted a mansion big as the Fairmont. The red columns were covered with carved animals painted gold.

All around the mansion he painted fountains and bridges and moon gates. Even when he had covered every square inch with lavish decorations, Mr. Pang wasn't satisfied.

"But I also wanted a banquet with a thousand fancy courses. I should have painted a bigger picture," he whined.

Grandfather sniffed at the open gates. "I think your banquet is inside. I can smell mushrooms frying."

Mr. Pang sniffed at the delightful smell. "Can I paint, or can I paint?" he declared proudly. "Now what do I do?"

"You step through it," Grandfather said.

Mr. Pang eyed the painting. "You don't hit the wall instead?"

"You saw us come out of it," Grandfather said.

As Mr. Pang continued to stare at the painting, Steve finally had a chance to warn him. "Your picture's very nice," he said. Actually, it wasn't, but Steve was too polite to say so. "But sometimes the brush can play tricks on you."

"So what?" As the brush dripped paint onto the floor, Mr. Pang examined his painting cautiously. Suddenly he held the brush like a sword and jabbed Steve. "You go first."

The Life of Luxury

"It's your painting," Steve argued.

"That's right. So any gold or jewels are mine," the landlord warned him.

Grandfather pulled Steve to the side. "I'll go first."

"Why?" Steve asked in surprise.

Grandfather looked hurt. "Do you really have to ask?"

"But I thought you didn't want me," Steve said.

"Where did you get that idea from?"

"Well, you're always scolding me, for one thing," Steve said.

"That was the way we were brought up," Uncle Fong explained. "There was an old saying back in China: Praise the child, spoil the child. Your grandfather was the happiest man in Chinatown when you were born."

"That's enough lovey-dovey," Mr. Pang said. "You can both go."

"All right, all right." Grandfather plunged through the window before Steve.

He really does love me, Steve thought as he followed him.

Uncle Fong came next. "Quit pushing, Pang," he said.

As they stood outside the mansion, a scandalized voice asked, "Sirs, what are you doing dressed like that?"

Steve saw a tall servant running toward them. His hair and eyebrows were blue. Behind him came a dozen servants. They also had blue hair and all wore satin jackets and pants embroidered with unicorns. In their hands they held fancy silk robes on which unicorns were also sewn.

Grandfather bowed politely. "We're just passing through," he said.

Uncle Fong turned in the direction of the window and said, "Pang, come on in. It's safe. Hey!"

"Sirs, you can't be seen in those rags," said Mr. Blue. At his signal the other servants pounced upon Grandfather and Uncle Fong and put unicorn robes on them right over their clothes.

The robes looked like they fit, but Grandfather complained, "This collar's too tight."

"Mine too." Uncle Fong tried to unbutton his collar.

"Sirs, important men must look important,"

Mr. Blue scolded. "These are all the latest fashion."
Gently but firmly he shoved Uncle Fong's hands away
from the collar.

Mr. Pang stepped through the painting with the
brush still in his hand. "Wait a moment. I'm the boss,"
he shouted. "Why are you dressing those bums in my
clothes?"

The puzzled servants whispered among themselves,
and then Mr. Blue turned to Grandfather and Uncle
Fong. "Sirs, if you don't mind, there's been a terrible
mistake."

Grandfather beat Uncle Fong at taking off his robe.
"It's quite all right."

"No, take mine," Uncle Fong complained.

"I'll take both," the greedy Mr. Pang said.

The next moment the servants had dressed Mr.
Pang in the robes, one over the other. They shrank
magically to fit him.

"Now let's eat," said Mr. Pang. He strutted like a
peacock toward the mansion.

"Sir, what are you doing?" Mr. Blue demanded in
shock. At his signal two dozen hands lifted Mr. Pang
high in the air.

Mr. Pang kicked his legs and flailed his arms. He
looked like a beetle on its back. "Hey, hey, put me
down," he ordered.

"Sir, what would the neighbors think if they saw
you walking?" Mr. Blue explained.

And the servants swept Mr. Pang over to a carrying chair. It was decorated with real gold and pearls. Next the servants slid jade-encrusted poles along the sides so the chair could be carried.

Mr. Blue shuddered. "Your feet should never touch dirt, sir."

Crouching beneath the chair poles, they lifted it onto their shoulders. Mr. Pang waved to Grandfather and Steve from behind a curtain on the side of the chair. "This is the life!"

As the servants carried Mr. Pang through the garden, Grandfather nudged Steve. "Let's follow and see what happens."

The servants carried Mr. Pang over bridges and through moon gates, underneath flowering trees and past fragrant beds of flowers.

They bore Mr. Pang through the doors of the mansion and right into a banquet room. The ceiling was so high, Steve could barely see the roof beams. Everything was decorated with gold and jade and pearls.

The servants carried Mr. Pang toward a huge table. It was groaning with golden plates and bowls. On them were fish and roast pigs and ducks. There were also a lot of dishes Steve didn't recognize.

"What's that?" he asked Grandfather, and pointed at a flat, pink something.

"I think it's pickled jellyfish," Grandfather whispered back.

"Ugh," Steve said.

"It's very tasty," Grandfather said. "A real China-towner is always willing to try a dish once."

Steve might try a nibble, but that would be the only time.

Mr. Pang sat down in a teak chair as big as a throne. It was carved like a dragon with silver claws. "I don't know where to begin," he said, smacking his lips.

"Sir." Mr. Blue frowned. "You can't look all messy like a common laborer. You must clean up."

And the other servants brought a large porcelain jar showing the many mansions and palaces in the sky. From the jar they poured water into a huge bowl decorated with the gardens of the sea.

"Yes, of course, I knew that." Mr. Pang laughed nervously. He handed the brush to Mr. Blue and allowed the other servants to wash him.

Steve, Grandfather, and Uncle Fong watched from the doorway. Mr. Blue brought the brush over to Steve and bowed. "Little sir, I believe this really belongs to you."

Steve noticed that the brush hairs matched the color of the servant's hair.

Steve hesitated. "I'm not sure I want it back. The brush plays tricks. You can't trust it," he said.

Mr. Blue smiled politely. "Little sir, magic cannot be tamed. Magic is like Nature. Can you control the rain? And do you blame it when it gets you wet and you catch cold? And yet does that same rain help your crops to grow and feed you?"

Grandfather looked thoughtful. "So we have to learn how to adjust to the magic. We have to survive the bad parts and enjoy the good."

Mr. Blue blinked his blue eyelashes. "I believe that's what I said, sir."

"But how much magic is left in the paintbrush?" Steve asked.

Mr. Blue chuckled. "How much rain is left in the sky, little sir?"

"I hate riddles," Uncle Fong groaned.

"The magic depends on you," Mr. Blue said, and glanced at Uncle Fong. "It depends on what you wish and how hard you wish."

"But I really wanted to see my parents," Steve said.

"You didn't let me finish," Mr. Blue said. "Wishing is only part of it, though. Magic is like riding the unicorn. Some of the time it will take you where it wants to go rather than where you want to."

Uncle Fong remembered his wish. "That seems like most of the time."

Mr. Blue faced Steve. "And, of course, you might outgrow the magic one day."

"I never will," Steve promised. Taking the brush, he hid it inside his sleeve and felt the hairs tickle him in greeting.

"We will see, little sir," Mr. Blue said. "Now if you'll excuse me, I have the master to serve." And with a polite bow, he returned to Mr. Pang's side.

As he wiped his hands on a silk towel, Mr. Pang smacked his lips. "Boy, oh, boy, am I hungry." He did not notice that he no longer had the paintbrush. "I'd like the beef with mushrooms. It's made me hungry just smelling it."

Mr. Blue shook his head. "Sir, you must have smelled our meal. That dish is only for common folk like us. You deserve far better fare." He clapped his hands.

From the kitchen marched a servant. In his hands was a silver tray. On the tray was a gold dish, and on the dish were things that looked like black chips. "The Twelve Friendly Funguses," Mr. Blue announced.

Mr. Pang pushed the dish aside. "Take it away! What else is there to eat?"

The servant looked disappointed as he removed the dish. He returned with a new dish.

"Snail Tails," declared Mr. Blue proudly.

"That's more like it." Mr. Pang eagerly picked up a pair of chopsticks.

"Sir!" Mr. Blue cried out, scandalized. He pried the chopsticks out of Mr. Pang's hand. "Please, allow me." Holding the chopsticks, he selected a tasty morsel and dangled it in front of Mr. Pang.

Mr. Pang opened his mouth like a baby bird, and Mr. Blue guided the Snail Tail carefully inside his mouth. A second servant cleaned Mr. Pang's mouth. A third put a hand on his jaw.

"Chew a hundred times, sir, to savor the flavor," Mr. Blue instructed.

Mr. Pang frowned and tried to pull free, but two more servants gripped him. As Mr. Pang began to chew, Mr. Blue kept count.

When he had chewed one hundred times, a sixth servant patted Mr. Pang on the back.

"Now please burp for us, sir," Mr. Blue requested politely.

Mr. Pang pounded the table. "This is ridiculous," he said, rising angrily. "I haven't lived sixty years to be treated like an infant."

When he tried to leave, the servants seized him and shoved him back into his chair.

Mr. Blue raised his hands in shock. "Sir, you haven't finished. You must eat the entire banquet."

Mr. Pang's eyes bulged. "Finish everything? And when is that?"

"When you've eaten all one thousand dishes," Mr. Blue informed him.

"I'll eat what I want, and I'll eat when I want," Mr. Pang shouted. He tried to get up again, but the servants held him down.

Another servant took the empty dish into the

kitchen and returned with a new one.

"Hump Stump of Camel," the servant cried happily.

"And don't forget, master," Mr. Blue reminded Mr. Pang. "Chew each bite one hundred times."

"But that will take forever," Mr. Pang wailed.

It was a mistake to keep his mouth open that long. A servant took the opportunity to shove a biteful of camel hump between Mr. Pang's lips.

Mr. Pang whipped his head from side to side. Then he tried to spit it out, but a servant clapped a hand over his mouth. "Chew, sir."

"And don't worry, sir. We have plenty of camel hump," Mr. Blue promised.

Mr. Pang tried to protest, but every time he opened his mouth, he was fed more camel hump. When he tried to get away, two servants pinned him to the chair.

Steve studied the next dish that a servant had brought. It looked like yellow-and-purple mush.

Steve started to feel sorry for the landlord. "Do you think we should help Mr. Pang?" he asked his grandfather and Uncle Fong.

Uncle Fong stopped him. "No, I think he's got more help than he wants right now."

Grandfather nodded. "But let's visit him later. Maybe he'll be more reasonable about things."

Steve grinned. Uncle Fong and Grandfather were much smarter than Steve had thought at first. "I guess we shouldn't interrupt his supper."

Laughing, they left the mansion and stepped out of the painting. And when they were back in their room, Steve painted shutters so they could shut out Mr. Pang's mansion.

The Rescue

That day they heard from the other tenants that Mr. Pang's family had come looking for him. Of course, they couldn't find any sign of him

The next night Steve examined the paintbrush. "I wonder how much we should trust the brush. The servant said it could be pretty quirky."

"Well, the Lady on the Moon was pretty good," Grandfather said, "until Mr. Pang interrupted it."

"Still, we don't know how it would have turned out," Uncle Fong said.

Grandfather glanced back and forth between the Moon Lady's window and Mr. Pang's window. "Maybe because some wishes are good ones and some are bad."

"What's so wrong with wanting to go home?" Uncle Fong demanded.

"Perhaps the paintbrush was trying to tell you that you can't ask for certain things," Grandfather suggested.

Uncle Fong scowled at him. "Paintbrushes aren't philosophers."

"But this came from my grandfather, and he was a kind of philosopher," Grandfather explained. "As a young man he had gone to a monastery to study a type of Buddhism called Ch'an. I think the Japanese call it Zen."

He gazed at the paintbrush. "My grandfather told me to pray that I would see a unicorn, because unicorns bring joy to the heart. I wonder if that applies to hairs from a unicorn's tail."

"What was joyful about returning to Dragon Back?" Uncle Fong demanded. "I've still got bumps from my sister's dumplings."

"You did enjoy parts of your trip," Steve said.

"And going there made you realize it's not what you really wanted," Grandfather pointed out.

"Help, help," they heard a faint voice.

Steve felt guilty. "That must be Mr. Pang. I'm surprised his family didn't hear him."

Uncle Fong shrugged. "Since they couldn't see him, they probably thought it was someone's radio in the distance."

"I guess we should do something," Grandfather said to Uncle Fong.

"I'll help you," Steve said, feeling relieved.

To their surprise even Uncle Fong agreed to help. "I'd better go along this time, too. Who knows what new tricks that paintbrush has in store for you?"

"You're getting soft, old man," Grandfather teased.

Uncle Fong drew himself up huffily. "It's nothing of the kind. I just don't want to have to break in a new pair of roommates. It's been hard enough with you two."

Uncle Fong didn't fool Steve anymore. "You're just like a crab. You're all hard on the outside, but you're mushy on the inside."

Uncle Fong tried to scowl, but his mouth turned up in a grin. "Nothing good is going to come from spoiling you this way. So don't blame me when you grow up rotten."

"I won't," Steve promised, and opened the shutters.

"Sometimes I forget what a good friend you can be," Grandfather said affectionately.

Uncle Fong waved his hand. "Enough already. Let's go." But when he thought they weren't looking, he wiped his eyes. Uncle Fong was as good as a real uncle.

Grandfather leaned his head toward the window. Then he cupped his hand behind his ear. "We should find out what's going on inside first. Maybe I can over-hear something."

"We can do better than that," Steve said. Getting out the paintbrush, he carefully painted a small window on the mansion. "Now we can peek inside at Mr. Pang."

Uncle Fong insisted on looking first. He started to giggle. "It serves the pig right."

Grandfather was next. He laughed too. "I heard the servant. Pang's only up to five hundred and three."

When Steve looked through the window, he saw Mr. Pang. He was so huge that he filled his chair. His fancy robes had split at the seams. And his eyes bulged like Ping-Pong balls.

"Please. No more. No more. Or I'll burst," he begged. His arms were tied to the chair with golden cords. He waved his fingers feebly. The banquet table was littered with empty bowls and plates.

The servants ignored him. They brought a golden platter. On it were a dozen odd-colored eggs. "Sir, here is five hundred and four: Hermit's Fungus over Peacock Feet. And remember: a hundred chews per bite."

"No, my jaws are worn out," Mr. Pang said, and clamped his mouth shut. However, one servant pried his jaws open while a second fed him.

"He looks like a balloon with little strings for arms and legs," Steve said. He felt a little guilty for leaving Mr. Pang there so long.

"But how do we get him away from his servants?" Grandfather wondered.

"I think I know how," Steve said. Quickly he painted a small, ugly black cloud. Lightning bolts bristled from the side like porcupine quills. Sheets of rain fell from it.

Leaning forward, he gently blew it right through

the tiny window he had just painted and into the mansion. Thunder rumbled and lightning flashed. They heard the servants shout frantically from inside, "Help! It's flooding in here!"

Uncle Fong patted Steve's shoulder. "How'd you get so smart? You couldn't have gotten it from your grandfather. It must be from your grandmother."

The three climbed through the window and ran into the garden. Streams of water poured out of the mansion. They struggled up the steps through the torrent.

Uncle Fong pulled his collar up. "Maybe you should have painted a smaller cloud," he said.

When Steve splashed through the doorway, he had to agree. Inside, the mansion was a mess. The cloud floated beneath the roof raining water below. Lightning flashed like bulbs on a camera. Then thunder boomed. He thought he was inside a huge bass drum.

On the walls away from the rain, fires burned. "Oh, no. Lightning must have started fires," Grandfather said.

The water was up to Mr. Pang's knees. He struggled to get up, but the cords held him to the massive chair. "Please help me," he called.

"Will you try to take my paintbrush ever again?" Steve asked.

Mr. Pang shuddered. "No, never. I don't want to ever see any brush ever. Not toothbrushes. Not hair brushes. Not shoe brushes. Nothing with any kind of brush."

Steve folded his arms. "And will you fix up the apartment building?" he asked.

Mr. Pang wiggled up and down on the chair seat. "Yes, yes. I'll make it nice as the Fairmont Hotel," he said desperately.

So Uncle Fong picked up a porcelain cup and broke it on the table. With the pieces they sawed at the cords. When they fell away, though, Mr. Pang could not stand up.

Grandfather scratched his head. "I don't think he can move fast enough to escape his servants."

Steve saw the carrying chair and pointed at it. "We can use that," he said.

Quickly they brought the chair over. However, Mr. Pang was so huge that he barely fit.

The three of them strained to lift the chair off the floor. "Maybe we should have saved him after only three hundred dishes. Now he's too heavy," Uncle Fong said, panting.

"No, no, don't leave me here," Mr. Pang moaned.

Slowly they waded through the water and out into the garden.

They saw the servants in the distance carrying piles of towels. They threw them down when they saw Mr. Pang trying to leave.

"Sir, sir! Come back! Where are you going?" Mr. Blue called.

Mr. Pang beat the sides of the chair. "Faster, faster," he shouted urgently.

"Oof," Uncle Fong puffed. "We're going as fast as we can. You try getting thinner, Fatty."

"Maybe we should just roll him along," Grandfather suggested with a chuckle.

Somehow they staggered to the window. The servants had almost caught up to them now.

Mr. Pang grabbed Grandfather and clung to him for dear life. "Don't let them take me," he wailed.

"Not if we can help it," Grandfather promised.

Steve and Grandfather each took an arm, and Uncle Fong took his legs.

"On three," Grandfather said. "Ready?"

When they nodded their heads, Grandfather counted, "One, two, three."

"Hurry," Mr. Pang said, looking behind them.

Together they heaved the landlord out of the chair. In the same motion they flung him toward the window. Mr. Pang's head and chest popped through, but not his hips.

"My sister's dumplings," Uncle Fong swore. "The pig's stuck."

Mr. Pang kicked his legs frantically. "Don't let them take me back."

"We'll have to shove him," Grandfather said. "On three again. One, two, three."

Together they lunged toward Mr. Pang. Their shoulders hit Mr. Pang at the same time. With a loud popping noise Mr. Pang fell through the window.

He gave a squeal each time someone climbed through the window onto him. When they were on the other side, Steve got a notebook and quickly wrote in it. Then he brought it back to Mr. Pang. "Here's a contract with all your promises. Please sign it," he said, and held out a pen.

Mr. Pang shook his head. All his chins wriggled. "I was under pressure."

Uncle Fong called through the window. "I forgot. Just how many dishes does he have to go?"

Mr. Blue appeared on the other side of the painted window. "The chef is very upset. He says the master will have to start over. Please come back, sir." The servants reached out for Mr. Pang.

Uncle Fong jerked his head at the servants. "So what will it be? Keep your promise, or go back?"

Mr. Pang shivered. "I couldn't eat the lizard gizzards again. Where do I sign?"

Steve held out his notebook. "Right here."

However, Uncle Fong grabbed it instead. "There's one more thing, though." And he scribbled a new promise on the contract.

Mr. Pang raised his head indignantly. "I will not wear a T-shirt that says I'm a greedy pig."

Uncle Fong picked up an ankle. "Enjoy your dinner

then. Steve, give me a hand, will you?"

Mr. Pang glanced at the window. Two dozen hands stretched through the window, ready to take him.

His eyes grew wide with fright. "I'm signing. I'm signing," he said, and wrote out his name.

Dancing on the Moon

The very next day an army of workers came into
the apartment building. They replaced the lights.
They painted the walls. They carpeted the floors.

The tenants gathered in the hallway to watch. "This
is Saturday. Do you know how much it costs to have
all these people work today?" a man said, scratching his
head.

"What's gotten into Mr. Pang?" a woman wondered.

Uncle Fong chuckled. "Maybe he got more than he
wished for."

Grandfather dug his elbow into Uncle Fong from
one side, and Steve nudged him from the other.

"Uh . . . or not," Uncle Fong said, rubbing his ribs.

Grandfather folded his arms as he watched all the
activity. "Maybe it won't be as nice as the Fairmont

Hotel, but it will be a lot better than it was."

The workers came over with paint cans and brushes and tried to go into their room. Grandfather hurriedly blocked the doorway. "That's all right. You just leave this room to us."

"Mr. Pang gave us special orders to do this room," the head painter protested.

"We'll take care of Mr. Pang," Grandfather said. Putting a hand on the painter's chest, he gently pushed him to the side.

When Uncle Fong and Steve had slipped into the room, Grandfather immediately shut the door. "Where should we go tonight?" he asked.

Uncle Fong stared at the two shuttered windows. "Maybe we should just let the workers cover them up."

Grandfather sighed. "I could do without Mr. Pang's window, but I would miss looking at our Chinatown moon."

"I'd miss the magic," Steve said.

Uncle Fong squirmed and muttered something. "What did you say, old man?" Grandfather demanded.

Uncle Fong shrugged. "I said that I'd miss the dreaming even more than the magic."

"It wasn't even the dreaming. It was the hoping," Grandfather said.

Uncle Fong grunted approvingly. "You're getting smarter the longer you hang around me."

"Maybe you're right. Maybe we'd better go back to

the way things were," Grandfather said.

Steve thought about their days before the paint-brush and felt like crying.

With a weary nod Uncle Fong got up. "I'll get the painters."

At that moment, though, they heard a nervous tap from behind the shutters of Mr. Pang's window. "Sirs, please don't do that."

Uncle Fong went over to the window and spoke through the closed shutters. "We've seen your kind of hospitality. Forget it."

"I understand if you don't want our leftovers," the voice said sadly. "It's not very fancy. It's just our humble fare."

Grandfather came over. "How humble?"

"It's only beef and mushrooms," the voice said.

"Did you say beef?" Before they could stop him, Uncle Fong had thrown open the shutters. On the other side of the window was Mr. Blue. He held a steaming bowl in his hands.

Uncle Fong took it and sniffed. "It smells heavenly," he said, and snatched it from Mr. Blue.

"I have another simple dish, too," Mr. Blue said, and started to bend over to get another bowl.

Grandfather caught Uncle Fong before he could sample his dish. "What's the catch? Is it going to give us pink stripes?" he asked Mr. Blue.

Mr. Blue looked hurt when he straightened. "Sir, we

only want to please you." He held out the second bowl. "Twice-cooked pork, sir?"

Uncle Fong eagerly shouldered Grandfather out of the way. "Now, we can't insult the fellow by refusing," he said, taking the pork dish in his hands.

As Mr. Blue raised a platter of steamed fish, he cleared his throat. "If I may be so bold, the Lady on the Moon has been quite upset. She expected you to visit again long ago."

"She did?" Grandfather asked wistfully.

"I have it on good authority," Mr. Blue replied, handing the platter to Grandfather with a bow. "I'll fetch the dirty dishes tomorrow morning, sir, when I bring you breakfast." And he closed the shutters himself.

At that moment they heard faint drumming from behind the moon window.

Steve got out the paintbrush. He felt the familiar tingle. "I think the paintbrush is trying to tell us that it's sorry."

Grandfather turned and asked them, "Well, what do you think?"

"I have done the safe thing all my life," Uncle Fong said, heading toward the window. "It's time to live a little."

"You hate the paintbrush's tricks. What if you wind up with pink polka dots?" Grandfather asked.

Uncle Fong turned so they could see his profile. "A handsome man looks good even in polka dots," he said.

When Grandfather opened the shutters to the moon window, they saw the Lady upon her porch.

"I have made some rice," she said, indicating a bronze bowl with a lid.

Grandfather cradled the dish. "We have only humble fare, my Lady."

The Lady lifted her head and sniffed the air. "But it smells delicious," she said.

Steve turned on the radio so that they would have soft dinner music. Then he, Grandfather, and Uncle Fong all stepped through the window. Together they dined on the moon. Even the Lady said she had never eaten better.

As Uncle Fong sat back, stuffed, he sighed with contentment. "The world always looks rosier on a full stomach."

The Lady sighed. "Some peaches would be so nice to finish off the meal."

Steve hated to disappoint her. "We know a place where there's some delicious ones. I could paint Dragon Back again."

Uncle Fong rubbed the bumps on his head from his sister's dumplings. "But the peaches are guarded by a she-dragon."

"A pity," the Lady said. "It's been so long since I've had peaches. If I even had a pit, at least I could plant it."

Uncle Fong coughed. "I have a pit."

The Lady smiled. "I would count it a great favor."

"Consider it done," Uncle Fong said gallantly. He climbed back into their room and brought back the little tin. "It will be worth the wait for the tree to grow."

"But the soil on my moon is magical," the Lady said, taking the pit from the tin.

When Uncle Fong had dug a hole, the Lady dropped it in and covered it up.

A green shoot poked up immediately. Uncle Fong sat down with a surprised plop. "Good heavens."

"My moon soil is almost as rich as Dragon Back's," the Lady said with a smile.

They watched as the shoot grew into a sapling, and the sapling into a tree. In a moment the tree's branches were bowing over with ripe peaches.

Trembling, Uncle Fong plucked one. "It's just like home."

Grandfather nudged him. "Ready to start dreaming again?"

Uncle Fong looked ready to cry. "I'm just so out of practice."

The Lady put her hand on his shoulder. "You'll learn."

With a bow, Uncle Fong presented the peach to the Lady. "For you, Lady."

She turned it over in her hands and sniffed it. "It smells delicious." And then she bit it. "And it tastes as good as it smells." She took another bite and laughed as the juice ran down her chin.

Uncle Fong picked peaches for the rest of them, and they were as good as those of Dragon Back.

After they had eaten their fill, the rabbit played a drum. Grandfather sang, and the Lady on the Moon danced.

As she swirled by Steve, she leaned over. "Look up, Steve."

He lifted his head to gaze up. There, in the black sky, their feet skipping over the stars, he thought he saw his mother and father dancing too, dancing just for him.

"They're not gone as long as you remember them," the Lady whispered, and drifted away.

And lying down upon the moon and staring up at the sky, Steve had never felt happier.

The next morning, when Steve woke, he felt his grandfather's arm around him. They were back in their bed. His grandfather and Uncle Fong must have carried him back. At first it had been strange to lie so close to Grandfather, but now Steve liked it.

Their room looked just as tiny and just as cramped as ever, but then he smelled dumplings steaming. He twisted his head to glance at the windows. The scent was coming from behind Mr. Pang's window. The dumplings would make a tasty breakfast.

And he could hear the Lady singing a cheerful tune behind the moon window. He wondered what other stories they could explore. When he went out into Chinatown, he was going to have to keep his eyes and ears open for more stories.

No, he was wrong. The room wasn't small after all. Nor was Chinatown. Grandfather had said: China-towners are made, not born.

Carefully Steve felt for the brush beneath his pillow and felt it tingle in greeting.

Across from them, he heard, Uncle Fong got up with a yawn. "Where do we go tonight, Steve?"

Grandfather sat up. "Let's each think about it today. We want to be careful."

Uncle Fong tapped his temple. "And crafty."

What had Mr. Blue said? Magic cannot be tamed. It was a wild unicorn ride. "And we also have to be ready to laugh," Steve said.

In his hand he felt the paintbrush stir, eager to open new worlds for them.

He couldn't wait either.

Made in the USA
San Bernardino, CA
12 February 2016

Harder Working Money

*How to Use Forward Thinking Retirement
Planning to Create Rushing Rivers of Passive
Income for Life*

Jay Leigeber

Table of Contents

INTRODUCTION

A Problem Worth Solving

It is reported that 95% of retirement plans are broken. Only 5% of Baby Boomers reaching retirement are prepared to fund the lifestyle to which their family has become accustomed for the remainder of their lives. This is a national travesty that will emerge over the next two decades.

Admitting the problem and taking proactive steps today is a worthy endeavor. I propose that for most people the current approach to retirement planning is unwinnable; however, there is an alternative that can be beneficial for most families. Sharing insights of this novel approach is the purpose of *Harder Working Money*.

A Journey of Discovery & Serving

Over the past several years, I've become captivated by the concept of **Harder Working Money**. This is a term I use for powerful wealth building and preservation strategies to accumulate a nest egg of assets that generates streams of passive income, a portfolio that will fully fund your retirement in less than one third of the time.

As I transitioned from the role of an employee in the corporate world to an entrepreneur, I wanted to learn ways that money can work harder, so ongoing personal efforts were less of a requirement. I desired a way out of trading time for money..

After all, a true definition of wealth is far more than just money—in my judgment, *freedom is about providing the opportunity to have greater choice in how I spend my time without undue limitation on the options available.* Money is only an enabler. When sufficient money automatically flows through your life, you are free to spend your time doing the things you truly enjoy, giving freely to others–pursuing activities that express your unique purpose. I believe bold purposeful action, aligned with your passions, will manifest true joy. When you are joyful you are stress free.

I am pursuing a journey of personal financial discovery and sharing insights from successes and set-backs. I desire to inspire others to take control of their own financial destiny and enjoy the lifestyle of their dreams.

I believe in thinking broadly and in challenging the status quo because I refuse to be a victim. Game-changing alternative strategies require *taking personal responsibility and control*—discovering unique solutions rather than just following the herd. I become incensed when I comprehend how the traditional game is rigged in favor of the institutions, rather than the people who earn and put up all the money. I've also become aware of some AMAZING techniques in wealth creation. I intend to share these insights and techniques with as many people as possible, solely from the desire to assist others achieve enlightenment and well-being. Consider it my way of serving and paying forward.

The premise of Harder Working Money is that powerful, yet little understood, financial strategies can dramatically impact long-term, compounded, after tax returns in ways that increase passive income and build wealth over time. Simply put, when your money is working harder, you have more pleasurable life choices and less stress caused by questionable finances.

As well, to build wealth quickly, it is essential to shift the risk/reward relationship to enjoy more lucrative returns, yet not take on undue risk. I perceive that advantaged opportunities typically occur in privately structured deals outside of mass markets. For centuries, the affluent have been aware of, and utilized, private investments not generally available to the masses, but this can change with broader awareness and taking personal control of your financial destiny. You, too, can discover how to participate in privately structured deals that shift the playing field to your advantage, so you, too, can achieve more in less time with less effort and risk.

Finally, it's not what you make—but what you keep and how quickly and reliably that you can make it grow that can transform your life. Net yields can be substantially increased when investments are conducted in a tax advantaged environment and when the hidden fees are exposed and eliminated. Learn new insights to become a master of EFFICIENCY. If you can double your rate of return, with efficient compounding, you can cut by two thirds the time it takes for you to reach sustainable prosperity. I believe this is a viable goal.

The clear purpose of Harder Working Money is to free up your time but keep your capital working as hard for you as possible, generating rushing rivers of passive income and capital preservation.

It's my observation that the average individual cannot achieve prosperity by working 9-5 and putting their savings in Wall Street or other traditional investment assets. Why? This approach takes far too long and requires too much savings out of your current active income.

You will discover there are private investment opportunities that consistently generate returns at 2, 5, and even 10 times the rates of general market returns, without corresponding increases in risk. There are asset classes that grow the stated amounts, regardless of the overall current economic trends. There are asset classes that shelter income in tax benefited ways, so you get all the cash flow income but pay tax on only a small portion of it, if at all. There are ways to avoid having the majority of your long-term gains in equity being stolen from you in excessive fees. There are uncommon techniques and hidden loopholes in the laws, which benefit the few who take advantage of what is offered and incentivized.

A few of the concepts in this book may surprise or amaze you. Others are things you are probably aware of but may feel have minor consequence; however, as will be exposed in reality, they have massive implications when considered over the long-term. That is a primary purpose in sharing my perspective on these concepts–helping you see the world of finance and investment opportunities in a new light and comprehend how your current choices are helping or hindering your chances of achieving prosperity or outliving your resources.

When you perceive things from an alternate perspective and comprehend new options/benefits, how you choose to manage your finances and what you choose to invest in may change. You will discover that intellectual capital and relationship capital can truly leverage monetary capital for personal benefit (what you know and who you know may be more important than how much money you currently have). But you will not likely find these novel opportunities presented to you by checking a box on a form your broker sends you or listening to his new recommendation on how to re-balance your current accounts. Discovering game changing

opportunities requires personal involvement, learning from new sources and taking direct control of your financial destiny.

If you receive all of your advice from Wall Street firms and their financial advisors—surprise, surprise—the only solutions and plans they recommend include self-serving securities. If you get advice from insurance companies—every recommendation will place a heavy emphasis on annuities. If you attend a real estate investment club, everyone seems hopped up on renting and flipping homes. Or if you spend time with entrepreneurs, they will suggest shunning traditional financial vehicles while leveraging development capital of risk tolerant investors to try to create new businesses. My point is not that any of these solutions are good or bad, just that when you are a hammer → every opportunity you perceive is a nail to be smashed with the tools of the trade you are most familiar with.

Smart investors obtain sage advice when planning; however, they also recognize the biases from each source and determine which advice is truly applicable to their current situation and goals. Every person has different interests, skills and risk tolerances. Some desire to be active in their investments, while others desire or need to be passive, because they either lack the time or the education to be an active investor. But that is OK…you can choose to be active or passive in either traditional investments or in the privately structured cash flow deals I advocate. You just need to find the game that is right for you.

You need to select investment concepts that make sense to you because, if you don't comprehend the offering, you are just shooting in the dark. When you are playing the wrong game, you will probably lose. When you discover your proper niche and use the right tools, everything can quickly fall into place, and you will feel more confident in your progress toward specific goals.

I am willing to freely admit my biases. You will notice consistent threads through this book that propose taking personal control of your education and financial planning and being an active investor. No other advisor can truly understand or look after your well-being as you are able to. When you get educated with the sage advice of mentors and advisors, but make the final investment decisions yourself with full comprehension of your options, you will be on a more proactive path to prosperity and protecting your family's financial well-being.

I seek personal control. Why be on a playing field where you can be disadvantaged by the system? I am biased to privately structured deals where risk and return can be shifted. After all, this is the only way to safely get ahead at a much quicker pace. Whether active or passive, you can learn how to participate in deals where the benefits are skewed to your side of the equation.

I have chosen to pursue recurring streams of passive income rather than focusing an amassing a huge amount of equity to draw down during my retirement years. To accomplish this, I am biased to real estate and private lending where each deal is unique and cannot be manipulated by the big financial players.

Rather than a pat scenario of asset class allocation and diversification, I prefer to focus on investments that I have experience in and am seeking to master.

My preferred solutions may or may not be relevant to you. Regardless, why should Wall Street fat cats and big banks get all the leverage off of your capital, while you take all the risk and are required to pay their exorbitant fees, win or lose? There are provocative messages covered herein that will benefit you no matter what type of investment environment you prefer.

The politicians and power brokers have set up our game board with certain rules and incentives. Most people are playing the game blind without understanding the rules. Only once you learn to read the tea leaves and observe how others are winning the game can you take full advantage of how the game can be mastered in far less time. Learn new strategies that enable you to be advantaged, going with the flow rather than swimming up-stream like salmon struggling to get to their spawning grounds.

This is why I recommend you get education/advice from a variety of sources and take personal control to generate a plan specifically aligned to your family's situation. Some of the investment techniques advocated will probably not be appealing to you. That is fine; all I ask is that you try to comprehend the advantages of these strategies and how they might be right for someone else. Then figure out the end point you are striving to achieve and utilize the best financial vehicle options to get you the results you are seeking.

Taking responsibility for your plan doesn't necessarily mean doing it all yourself. Just evaluate a number of options and decide which investment sectors will be most efficient to achieve your specific desired end point. Then research and select the right team, whether you choose to play an active role or a passive investor role.

Pursuing alternative investment strategies may require moving your retirement account into a self-directed IRA, so you can expand the array of options to a basis much greater than traditional Wall Street vehicles. Or it may require setting up your own personal Family Bank so you can recapture much of the interest expense that flows through your normal everyday life. These are concepts that are probably foreign to you now, but I'll help to explain how they can benefit you in achieving your financial goals in less time, with less risk.

Once you have investable capital beyond your family's current lifestyle expenses—you too will benefit by comprehending the financial leverage principles the affluent have used for centuries to preserve and compound generational wealth. You, too, can enhance your path to financial freedom. If you are dedicated to following the plan over time, you, too, may be wildly successful in creating legacy wealth that future generations will appreciate.

I'm concerned that too many people feel like victims in an economic scenario that seems out of control and unwinnable. Too many people seem to be fearful of outliving their money during retirement. My purpose is to illuminate new insights, to inspire people what is possible and share novel investment techniques, which enable prosperity in a relatively short period of time.

Too many people also fail to make long-range financial plans, leaving their future liquidity and lifestyles up to chance. It is only through direct control of your education, planning and implementation that you will find the best solution for your unique situation. Your family's long-term well-being is at stake; shouldn't this become your top priority?

Many people do not fully comprehend how much the game of finance has changed. We may have "learned the rules" when we watched how our grandparents or parents retired with a defined pension plan that gave them income for life. Yes, we understand that, now, many of us have been forced into 401K plans, but nobody really took the time to educate us on how to manage our retirement funds and prepare for the personal responsibility that has been placed on us. Now is the time to fill that void before you are in a distribution phase without realistic options.

Many of my Baby Boomer generation are just waking up to the fact that, after the market crashes of 2000 and 2008, our retirement

savings may be far from where we need them to be for a secure retirement, even after "doing the right thing" of maxing out 401K contributions and keeping funds in an array of mutual funds that may have not been growing the way we need them to. What is a concerned person to do? Why not get educated on new options that can be real game changers?

Regardless of your age or current financial situation, seeing things from alternate perspectives can benefit your comprehension and behavioral choices. It's never too late to broaden one's perspective, make sound choices and direct one's financial results toward a specific purpose. Others have opened my eyes; I hope to shine a bright light and give you a clarifying lens that helps you perceive finance in a distinctive way that can dramatically improve your financial destiny. Clarifying options and defining a plan won't eliminate all risk, but at least it will help you comprehend the path you are on and how external conditions are helping/hurting your progress toward your goals, so you can correct your course along the way.

The information in this book is NOT meant to provide any specific answers for your financial situation or challenges. I don't know your unique situation or personal desires. I am not your investment advisor—just a person striving to protect his family's retirement lifestyle by becoming an educated, active investor. However, awareness of the principles and insights I have formed may help you begin to ask new questions and formulate new plans from a new paradigm. Like me, you can begin to learn of new options and benefits from a variety of people who have chosen the alternative investment path. Hopefully, with a broader awareness, you will become more secure in the choices you are making.

What does the future hold? I believe the next 20-30 years are going to be fundamentally different than recent decades. If you are only crafting your plans and strategies based on your prior experience or

following game plans developed in a different era, you are likely to be shocked as our future emerges with new challenges and opportunities.

Part of the message shared may be perceived to be negative. That is not my intent; overall *I am very optimistic about what is possible for people who make purposeful plans and implement them*. I am a strong believer in a person's ability to step up and handle any challenge he or she becomes passionate about and is committed to overcoming. However, it is prudent to face the honest economic facts in which your personal investment plan needs to work.

Our country's debt is growing exponentially, with no sound solutions to stem the flow or begin to pay it back. Unsustainable levels of debt will have practical implications on the economy moving forward, and to ignore it is foolish. Since the national debt obligations cannot affordably be serviced with "normal" interest rates, politicians and power brokers will strive to hold them very low for the foreseeable future. In the near term, this will likely have negative implications on the returns on traditional safe investment options. Some consider this a war on savers, but you can choose to avoid the loser's game by developing other investment options that can safely yield an attractive return on capital with reasonable risk.

If you expect others to take care of your finances, you are likely to end up with a big surprise, playing an unwinnable hand. It is essential that each of us to take personal responsibility for managing our current earning, spending and saving patterns to adequately fund the retirement lifestyle we desire. We all need basic financial education and to learn of all available strategies to effectively fund our retirement. Then after we accumulate this nest egg, we need to securely manage it through a volatile market so it isn't all diminished by downswings in market cycles. Great

investors always place great focus on protecting the downside, as well as pursuing the upside. This book covers several risk mitigation techniques.

Unfortunately, I believe too many people are unprepared for their financial responsibility. Hopefully, the insights and information contained herein will be the jolt needed to get a few people to choose a new path forward, causing them to become educated and select strategies that are prudent for their family's well-being and aligned with their interests and skills. If you are energized by some of the information and investment techniques shared in this book, I've succeeded in my quest. I'm certainly not suggesting my choices should be your choices. I only want you to be aware of many choices that are likely off of your radar screen...and to comprehend one person's views of why these options are attractive in specific ways.

While I was moving up rapidly in corporate America and living the good life, I had little interest in or concerns about taking direct control of my family's financial future. Life seemed easy and abundant, so I just went with the flow. Through job displacement, I went through a jolt, as all of that security was taken away.

Now that I'm an entrepreneur, discovering a Plan B path to financial prosperity has become my passion. Since I'm aware there is so much fear about finances amongst my peers, my purpose is to share novel concepts that may help others see a brighter picture of possible prosperity as well. Perhaps you will figure out your own responsible Plan B before you face challenges without it. No one will tell you the path of personal control is easy...but in my judgment, this journey of education and altering choices is necessary for the security of your family's lifestyle.

Who Will Benefit by Reading This Book?

If you desire to learn the strategies of when, where and how to build wealth, I have a non-traditional message to share. I've spent the past several years evaluating options and have clarified my personal plan. I believe this is a forward thinking approach to retirement planning. My plan rejects the traditional memes society taught us about the proper path to prosperity.

When I decided to share these insights in the hopes that they could help others, I had a specific audience in mind. I feel an affinity with successful people who are nearing the time of retirement but don't feel prepared. Just as I was a few years ago, many people want to do the right and responsible things for their families and realize they need a better plan. They are successful or experts in one aspect of their lives but have not necessarily been exposed to /become experts in how to succeed in long-term financial planning. One day we wake up and recognize there could be significant risk in this one area of our life. We begin to seek answers to many questions.

Many are concerned about how to grow their nest egg so they will be able to pay for their children's college and weddings, as well as carry them through the retirement years. Perhaps they feel it's hard to know our country's real economic situation when the mainstream news headlines are so provocative in the area of Wall Street's greed and its effect on individual financial planning and success. Perhaps they have come to realize they should control their own money rather than turning it over to 3rd parties who have their own priorities and focus. Perhaps they have extra earnings to invest; however, they don't know how or where to put them so they don't put the funds at too much risk and, yet, have the chance of generating a reasonable reward.

Much of the information people see on the news, on the internet or read in books seems contradictory, but this is to be expected. All advisors/experts have biases; it's up to you to understand where each of these sources is coming from and why their world view is what it is. Then you must decide what your world view will be and build your plan off of the foundation of your own paradigm.

"Save" Your Marriage

Not seeing eye-to-eye on family financial matters is a major cause of relationship stress. While one partner may be the primary earner or planner in the family budget it is critical that all parties get on the same page on spending and investing. When there is joint agreement on the necessity and parameters of the family budget and long-term retirement plan, everyone can work together to overcome challenges and celebrate successes. They can pull together to invest what is necessary for long-term lifestyle benefit.

I am happy to share that Gale and I have been married for 40 years. We have faced several challenges along the way but are both optimistic that our Harder Working Money plan will succeed. We are looking forward to the time and financial freedom that we anticipate enjoying for the remainder of our lives.

Note: While I do have an MBA and 30 years' experience in managing huge consumer packaged goods brands, I'm not a certified financial advisor, nor am I formally educated in economics. *I've simply become an individual captivated by strategies of wealth creation and preservation traditionally used only by the select few.*

The ideas expressed herein are not my own; I'm sharing the insights that I've gained by reading scores of books and getting trained by several experts in the real estate and entrepreneurial business building sectors. Certainly, I believe I have something to offer beyond the original source material. Over the past 5 years, I've executed several dozen privately structure deals, and I'll be happy to share my insights from deals that went well and those I wish I had a do over on.

Please realize I am not your fiduciary and am certainly not providing investment advice for others. I have nothing to sell, just a point of view to share. While I have attempted to be accurate throughout this book, realize it's just one person's perspective. I have no legal/tax or financial certifications.

Won't you join me on this journey of discovery? Together we can all form new insights and help each other gain control and succeed in our journey to financial prosperity. If you would like to discuss any topics covered herein, just reach out to me at Jay@HarderWorkingMoney.com. One of the purposes in publishing this book is to connect with like-minded people on their own journey of transformation, in the hope that we can help each other succeed.

Chapter 1—THE OBSTACLES OF WEALTH CREATION

The ability to design an effective wealth creation plan depends on clearly understanding the situation and defining key issues to solve from the perspective of your own family's situation. This section is not intended to alarm, merely to build a platform of comprehension and insights upon which realistic, long-term plans and solutions can prevail.

In an environment where we have been forced into 401K's, where tax burdens are skewed, where certain behaviors are incentivized and we all are challenged by the hidden tax caused by the devaluation of our dollar…we must realize that the *threshold for funding the retirement of our desires is likely to be much higher than most anticipate*. The magnitude of the challenge is why facing facts and building a realistic plan is so essential. Additionally, the advances in medicine that extend longevity imply that our distribution period in retirement may be much longer than currently anticipated. Rather than a retirement plan needing to fund 10-15 years, today one should plan on double that or more. In other words, the problem to solve regarding not outliving our resources in retirement is a VERY BIG NUMBER.

If your retirement investments are in a distribution taxed traditional IRA or 401K, the required nest egg to maintain your lifestyle through a longer retirement is probably well over $1,000,000 for a modest lifestyle—certainly multiple millions if you've been successful and enjoy a lifestyle well beyond what is possible for the masses.

Is your current financial plan on track to achieve this magnitude on a timely basis? If so, congratulations, you are one of the few percent of the population ahead of the game. If not, are there optional approaches for you to consider that don't require such a massive nest egg, yet can sustain the lifestyle you desire? Certainly...*if I didn't have a hopeful message to share, I wouldn't be trying to explain the concepts behind Harder Working Money*.

Reports suggest that the recommended portfolio hurdle is over eight times what the average Baby Boomer holds when reaching retirement age. This implies too many people are heading for very challenging lifestyle choices in retirement. With proper planning and action today, you have the opportunity to improve your long-term standing, regardless of your current situation. Figure out a plan that has a chance of success and pursue it with vigor.

Different people face different challenges to winning the prosperity game. This is why each individual needs to take personal control and figure out a plan that works for their unique situation. Achieving prosperity for your own family is really all that should matter to you.

If you are in a positive position of being closer or "on plan" for your current life stage—how do you preserve and protect that which you have worked so hard to accumulate during this current environment of high market volatility and slow economic growth? Can you rely that the strategies that worked to put you in this favorable situation will maintain their effectiveness moving forward? Are you protecting your downside risk?

On the other hand, if you are behind in your savings plan, you cannot change the choices you have made over the past several decades or what has happened to you up to this point. But from this point forward, with education/planning/action, you can decide

what to do with every next dollar you make and how a portion of it can begin to create a better financial future for your family. Commit to taking personal control and educating yourself today. Commit to implementing the tough choices you can make today to improve your situation tomorrow.

The following example may enlighten how dramatically our environment and economy changes. Forty years ago, our grandparents were likely alive, perhaps in the formative stages of funding their retirement or in the midst of their golden years. At that point, could they ever imagine what our lifestyles would be like today...or the prices we would be paying for everyday expenses? I recall when nice family homes were selling in the $20-40,000 range, fully equipped family sedans sold for $2,500-5,000, and gasoline was under $.35 a gallon. If these were the assumptions they built their retirement plan on, how could they be surviving today if they are blessed and still alive? Your current annual tax burden is likely many times what your grandfather earned in a year. Life was different then, and the dollar went much further. Today, some prices are up 10X. Perhaps they enjoyed a pension that kept them current to the rising cost of living and growing health care expenses. If not, they may have had to make difficult lifestyle decisions or become a financial burden on others.

I bring this up to suggest that *inflation has become a constant in our lives and the long-term impact is substantial*. It is foolish to plan for decades of retirement solely based on today's cost of living. Think broadly about how to build an investment portfolio that benefits from annualized growth beyond the anticipated historical levels of inflation. This is the only way to preserve the purchasing power of the money you save in retirement accounts. How can you own assets that grow in value more than the cost of inflation or the speed at which the dollar devalues? How can you

generate recurring streams of passive income that continue regardless of market cycles or swings in our economy?

Compounding our financial challenge today is the fact that too many Americans remain buried by a mountain of debt and are struggling to maintain their lifestyle while working—let alone saving/investing to sustain that lifestyle once their active income stops. The average American is saving less than 5% of his or her income and most of his or her investments are delivering long-term returns under what the traditional retirement plan assumptions have been calculated on. Without a more aggressive savings or investment plan to accumulate and grow one's retirement nest egg more aggressively during one's working years combined with a debt reduction plan, one may be confronted with outliving his or her savings.

Most American families are rolling over consumer debt every month, and many are just paying the minimal payments required. Do they realize the extent of current income in their family budget going toward interest? Assuming one is carrying a modest balance on credit cards and has a mortgage and a couple of car loans, interest expense often exceeds one third of all available after tax income!

This is a very heavy load to carry from every month's budget, and it squeezes out the opportunity to save. If you are prudent in budgeting and paying down debt by just a handful of percentage points, this freed up cash flow can be redirected toward investments. And for the fortunate few who learn to set up their own private Family Bank, they will recapture this interest expense in their own financial balance sheet, rather than paying it to disinterested 3rd parties. This simple change can initiate a virtuous spiral of retirement savings growth, rather than an ever-increasing debt burden of doom.

Solutions start with awareness of the situation and a plan to enable a different future state. Small amounts of debt reduced or savings invested and compounded over a few decades can amount to very substantial outcomes. Some of the math we go through later in this book will probably astound you. That is why I take the time to go through it, so the picture becomes clear, and you can choose to make more effective financial decisions.

My overall point in this section is that *the "average American" is playing a losing hand*. Too much income is going to interest due to excessive purchasing on credit. Without structuring for advantage, too much of people's income is going to taxes. Investing in typical Wall Street financial vehicles, too much is going to fees, while at the same time, investors are receiving lower than necessary returns while experiencing above necessary market volatility risk. And finally compounding all of these problems is the fact that the US dollar is losing substantial purchasing power year after year. The result of all of these factors implies the magnitude for extensive retirement savings is ever growing, yet most people's retirement portfolios are growing at very meager rates beyond their savings contributions. I believe once you realize something is broken, you should attempt to FIX IT.

You don't need to be that "average American." If you decide to alter your approach and start playing a different financial game, perhaps your outcomes can be far better than the average Joe that is just hoping things work out in the long run or burying his head in the sand. You can begin to save more. You can start to invest in deals you understand. You can learn to grow your accounts at higher rates in tax sheltered environments. You can learn to eliminate unnecessary fees. You can begin to follow a plan with a better chance of success.

Let's be clear in our focus. While it might be altruistic, we, individually, can't help solve the problems of the masses. Maybe

the government can help all the other people, but to date I perceive their efforts have been counterproductive and filled with unintended consequences. But *what we can commit to do is define and safeguard our own plan, protect our own family*. We can start to make choices today that are aligned with a clear path toward prosperity.

Forward thinking retirement planning can allow us to choose an alternate path and make changes today that could greatly enhance our family's chances to afford a desirable lifestyle through our 80's/90's and perhaps beyond.

Doing well is a noble thing, not something to be despised. Those who are fortunate in life are in a much better position to meaningfully give to those in true need. Those who do well create growth in our economy that helps everyone be better off. Those who do well can leave a legacy for future generations of loved ones.

It is prudent to take personal responsibility and control to protect our own families. We should accept the responsibility to educate our families and loved ones of a better way to earn, spend and invest—to understand and leverage powerful financial principles. While others may be doomed to suffering unpleasant choices in the future because of lack of planning and neglect, as long as we become committed to taking bold, purposeful action today, we can change our family's financial destiny. We can choose to start saving more of our current income in high yielding assets, invest in assets that grow in an inflationary environment and focus on generating multiple streams of passive income. That is the path I have chosen for specific reasons outlined in this book. Perhaps you will choose to join me on this alternative path to prosperity.

Welcome to Uncertain Times

In early 2015, while this was being written, we all face financial obstacles to wealth creation including a slow recovery from the recession of 2008, government practices that continue to put up roadblocks and bubble markets that give and then take away equity in securities and housing. Add to that scant new full-time job prospects and wages that don't seem to keep up with inflation. Young and old, today more people seem confused and daunted about the proper pathway to financial security.

I believe those who trust that companies or the government will care for them are risking their future finances to chance with very low odds of success. Today, retirement planning has fundamentally changed, and the environment in which your plan must prevail is turbulent.

Since the 80's, most companies have shifted the retirement burden to their employees—from defined benefit pension plans where the company was responsible for funding a lifetime of benefits → 401K programs where every individual is responsible for his or her own financial destiny. Sure your employer probably gives you a small matching contribution each year; however, the responsibility for managing, growing and adequately funding the account is totally up to you. Are you comfortable in your new role? Do you feel qualified to make sage decisions? If not, what are you doing to educate yourself and take prudent action while there is still time left on the pre-retirement clock? I congratulate you on taking the step to see if what I have to share is meaningful/helpful to you.

With regard to Social Security and Medicare entitlement programs, while these must be considered as a part of an every retirement plan, in my judgment, one should not assume that they will be sufficient to protect one's lifestyle and well-being. Social Security was initially set up to be a supplemental retirement program, not to

fully pay for recipients' full lifestyles. Similarly, Medicare was designed to fill a specific role in the healthcare of our seniors, but not to be a one-size-fits-all funding answer to every healthcare expense. Most people nearing retirement age have no full understanding of these programs or of the expenses that are likely to be required beyond their benefits. How can you create a realistic plan if you don't know all the tools in your toolbox? I suggest you learn more about these programs before they become a part of your life.

Unless these entitlement programs are changed or taxes are raised dramatically, the one thing we know is that they could soon drive our government to the brink of insolvency. It's indisputable math. The number of people contributing is growing much slower than the number of people receiving benefits. Over the next several years, monthly outlays for Social Security will grow over $80 billion per month when the full impact of Baby Boomers is felt. That is a trillion more a year in unfunded entitlements. And Medicare is an even larger liability. The way these programs are set up, many recipients are getting back multiple times what they contributed. Typical of government programs, they are set up to transfer wealth from one generation (the young) to another (the elder). Our politicians have not put away the funding required for these entitlements in a lock box. They have spent the resources to fund current bureaucracy, social programs and wars. Since the government's entitlement programs are meager and underfunded, how will you step up to protect your future where you are totally responsible for your family's financial well-being?

If you are fortunate in achieving a modicum of financial success, you need to find ways to preserve wealth, as many in society feel successful people should give most of it back in taxes. And given the dramatically growing unfunded liabilities, certainly taxes are likely to go up in the future for everyone. But taxes are not levied

on a universal and even basis. Some activities are incentivized, others highly taxed. If you structure your financial house with a firm tax advantaged foundation, your net earnings can compound faster, and your future distributions can be magnified. With tax efficiency, our money can work harder. *It is essential to get expert guidance in tax efficiency to achieve financial freedom.*

Real success isn't about earning a high income relative to the masses. This may be challenging for successful professionals to fully comprehend. When you are achieving career success as a manager or private business practitioner, you may think that you are winning the game. Sure you may be living a wonderful lifestyle now, but are you achieving this with limitations on personal debt? Or like so many Americans, has the appeal of easy credit influenced you to really live beyond your means? Is your retirement account savings growing adequately to be able to sustain this lifestyle? Have you been transitioning active income into sustainable passive income stream assets? What will happen when you stop work and the active income flow stops? Isn't it past the time you should have started to develop an exit Plan B, even if you are decades from retirement?

It's reported that only about 5% of the Baby Boomer population is prepared with a funded retirement plan that will be able to sustain their lifestyle through the remainder of their lives. The average Baby Boomer has saved $120,000 in their 401K when they have reached retirement. At a 4% disbursement/year that equals $4,800/year, out of which you need to still pay taxes. To this, Social Security would add a current average of $15,500/year. What type of lifestyle can $20,300/year provide for your family? Will you be able to maintain your lifestyle on that? Even if your current total is 2X or 4X the average—what does this imply on your future lifestyle choices? And what happens should inflation grow more than your retirement account?

Although you may not be where you desire to be today, don't settle for diminished expectations. Choose to do something about creating a better future while you still can.

There is only one type of thinking that can support our efforts to succeed in generating lifelong prosperity. That is *a positive, can do attitude of personal responsibility*. I take significant encouragement from the many people I've become aware of that have become financially free in less than a decade. What do they have that's different from the rest? I notice a will to win and an expectation that the proven paths of others will direct them to their desired outcomes. They are willing to decide and commit to a plan, then act boldly. Their successes have magnetized my desires and commitment.

I believe anything is possible for you if you just open your mind to novel options, take time to educate yourself, align with the proper partners and then take appropriate purposeful action. But time is of the essence; in all likelihood, to have a realistic chance of hitting your targets, you may need to alter your path today. That implies you need to figure out your retirement plan NOW and begin implementing your new strategies this year. Perhaps the information in this book will help you get off to a good start.

The encouraging news is that people with far less advantage than I, have built substantial wealth and future security by taking personal control at the appropriate time. On my journey of enlightenment, I've run across hundreds of people that are well on their way to building life altering passive income streams. This isn't necessarily something that takes decades or starts with a huge bank account. Just by starting to get educated and taking action now, in ways that are aligned with the best returning investment options of the moment, you too can be on a planned path to prosperity.

It has been stated that there are more millionaires made in times of strife than when everything seems to be going well. A challenging environment can be a blessing for those who know what they are seeking and are educated on how to take advantage of troubling times. I, for one, intend to be on the winning side of this situation in our current chaotic environment. Won't you choose to join me?

To change your results, change the rules/change your thinking. You need to become informed of options you probably don't even realize exist. Awareness and utilization of new strategies enable deploying capital in ways that work much harder, so you enjoy broader choices in how you spend your time and the quality of your lifestyle. In other words, with the proper strategies, *your money works hard so you won't have to*! Open new doors of possibility, so you can enjoy life more, leaving worry and stress behind.

I am advocating an alternate, positive perspective filled with abundance and possibility. I propose the best solution generally involves leveraging intellectual capital and relationship capital as much as financial capital. Through subtle changes in investment strategies and practices, you can leverage your finances and take advantage of opportunities around you that few are aware exist. You can choose to join with others who are structuring private deals that provide significant advantage.

Even if the overall economy is stalled, you can *create your OWN ECONOMY, providing opportunities for consistent growth and expecting that your family will prosper*. You can also limit your fair tax burden so you keep more of what you earn. If you start now, it is possible to control assets and build streams of passive income today, as well as build long-term equity to afford the retirement lifestyle of your dreams down the road. It's happening for me and can happen for you as well.

A Challenging Environment to Build Wealth

We live in a chaotic & confounding economy and, therefore, knowing how to get ahead financially is more difficult than ever. The old rules and practices may not apply today.

During the 2nd half of the 20th century, investing seemed easy. Just ride the stock market up and discover that equity in your house kept growing too. Sure there were cyclical setbacks about every 4-8 years, but shortly thereafter, the economy seemed to roar ahead and quickly be in positive territory again. Often, the gains on the rebound were massive. Certainly, the long-term trends were positive, and many people just did the same things as all of their friends and saw their net worth go up substantially. In that time, it didn't seem critical for me to define a personal wealth building plan because everything seemed to be working so well in my life. Perhaps easy success made me lazy, expecting it would always be this way.

The recent experience of the bull market in the 80's and 90's should be perceived with a clearer historical perspective to broaden awareness and highlight possible risks. After all, this was the time when so many employees were forced out of pension plans and into 401K plans. And where did all this money go? It went into the stock market—the only choice provided. Many pundits believe the market gains of these decades were primarily driven by the influx of all this new money pouring in. At any rate, we must be cautious of projecting this same kind of growth moving forward, unless similar conditions with new influxes of capital will replicate.

Those who perceive this cautionary tone as being Chicken Little will claim that all is well. After all, we've come out of the recent recession, and the stock market has made record gains, up about 130% since the bottom. But was all this growth driven by sound productivity improvements by businesses and income gains by the

masses saving more money in the market? Or was this bull market also artificially driven, this time manipulated by the government printing trillions of dollars that are artificially propping up the market in a bubble? It matters from the standpoint of sustainability and likely future volatility of the markets. Today, following the herd and putting more and more money into stocks may be analogous to following lemmings about to go over the cliff.

Realize the stock market is very volatile. During the 2000's there were two occasions when the market had major declines of up to 50%. Jack Bogel, CEO/founder of Vanguard Funds predicts we should prepare for two more such declines in the next decade.

The intelligent investor should seek out independent insight and perspective from broad-minded individuals who understand how wealth is created and how downside risks can be mitigated. Don't be dismayed by the doom and gloom predictions of catastrophe, but try to comprehend their arguments. Their conclusions may be misconstrued, but they also point out potential risks to be aware of/dealt with.

I prefer to dwell on the positive messages by futurists predicting new sources of abundance driven by emerging technologies—and try to figure out how they can positively impact my personal lifestyle.

New awareness from all sides allows a paradigm shift, so you can build your financial plan around assumptions that are more realistic of what you believe you will be facing 20-30 years from now, rather than planning for the current tenor of the times.

I advocate educating yourself from a variety of sources and follow your intuition of the best prospects for your success. One can never be certain about the future, but if you have studied available options and made choices aligned with your specific situation, you

are more likely to move in the direction of your desires. Just like in Robert Frost's poem "The Road Not Taken," there often may be many benefits to pursuing the alternative path few go down. *I've always been interested in what the successful do that the masses do not*. I have chosen an alternate path, attempting to make my money work much harder by following in the footsteps of people I have learned to admire.

Is Our Economy Experiencing Fundamental Shifts?

How is our broad financial context changing? Historically, America's economy thrived because of cheap credit, cheap energy and cheap commodities. Our nation became the bread basket of the world, and our entrepreneurialism and technological innovation set America apart. Today, with developing nations across the globe competing for capital, energy and commodities, the prices of certain limited resources are going up and will likely continue to do so over the rest of our lives.

But it's not all bad news. Other prices unexpectedly drop, for example the recent new affordability of petroleum-based products. Today, the entrepreneurial spirit is exploding across the globe. I believe we are experiencing a global shift in power, and you can either be a participant in it or get run over by it.

Certainly, there is no current nation or economy that can compete with the US on a per capita basis (all Americans are blessed to be here); however, emerging competition is clearly having an impact on our ability to rebound out of market cycles. The impacts of rising prices and cost of living should be considered as you develop your personal wealth building strategy. To me, it seems reasonable to assume that the future growth of America's economy as a whole may have lower growth rates than have been the case in

the past century. This is one reason I believe *it is essential for you to do everything possible to plan your own financial destiny, rather than just expecting you can ride the rising tide of a prosperous US economy*.

Key financial experts I follow believe the US economy is likely to be in a deflationary environment for the next decade. The velocity of money (turnover of all the money in the US economy) has been plummeting since 1997, driven by increasing monetary supply and modest real growth. The government can continue to print currency, but if people are not borrowing it for productive purposes, there is low compounding of value creation, which is what really drives our economy. The theory goes that since there is so much debt supporting these inflated asset prices, should values crash, debt will go into default creating deflation. Debt can be good when it is productive debt (increases velocity); however, it is bad when it is non-productive (decreases velocity). Today the velocity of money levels is at cyclical lows. I perceive this to represent risk.

However, the rising value of the dollar, relative to other world currencies, implies an influx of foreign investment, as world investors are seeking stability and even though the US economy is in a slow muddle through wave. Everything is relative, and many still perceive the US as the safe haven for protecting wealth on a global scale when there are so many troublesome economies around the world today. I perceive this to represent opportunity.

During 2015, when this is being written, the US stock market has risen to record highs while the volatility index of the market is relatively low. Yet many speculate it is actually a billowing bubble ready to pop. Some believe the next crash will be a devastating reset rather than just a normal market cycle correction because of all of the government intervention with TARP and successive attempts at quantitative easing. They predict a market crash that

could wipe away over 50% of the current market valuation within the next couple of years. Is your downside adequately protected should such dramatic market losses occur?

Even if you consider an extreme decline in the stock market a remote possibility, how would substantial market volatility impact your financial future if your entire portfolio is tied to the Wall Street roller coaster? Do you have the time it may take over the next decade to recoup from setbacks before your impending retirement years when you need to start distributing what you have accumulated? Are there options to protect your capital from market crashes and preserve your security? Should you leave the majority of your funds tied to this volatile, risky market?

Another moderating factor on future stock market valuation to consider is the fact that the majority of Baby Boomers have their retirement funds set up in 401K/IRA's in stocks and bonds tied to Wall Street. As they begin to sell off assets to pay for their retirement lifestyle expenses—and these plans require mandatory distributions so the deferred taxes can be paid— will there be sufficient investment demand by the younger generations or foreigners to support current market valuations? Prices are always a reflection of supply versus demand.

Isn't it reasonable to assume that there will likely be more sellers than buyers in the mass market financial vehicles over the next couple of decades as Baby Boomers shift from the accumulation phase of their lives to the distribution/lifestyle maintenance phase? Certainly, most wealth is held by people in and near retirement. To me, it seems only natural that this forced selling may have downward pressure on market prices over the next 20 years, simply because of demographic factors. How many in the younger generations do you know who are aggressively accumulating stocks versus focusing on paying down their student debt?

Traditional "safe" investment assets such as treasuries and CD's or money market funds are providing minimal historic yields as the Federal Reserve policy is holding short-term rates at near zero return levels. Prognosticators suggest this may remain the case for years, if not decades, to come because our government can't afford to pay higher interest rates and they set the rates.

Ultra low interest rates are particularly troublesome to seniors who often rely upon fixed income and want to avoid general market risks. Even if one has a portfolio of $1,000,000 in their retirement account, if CD's are paying less than 2%, how could one possibly live on $20,000 a year pre-tax? Will they need to draw down principal at a far greater rate than the recommended 3-4% per year? What are the implications of this type of distribution reality on the possibility of outliving one's resources?

And what will happen to the value of current bonds should interest rates finally begin to rise? Current bond valuations will plummet. Those with holdings will be stuck for the long-term with low yield assets or will need to take substantial hits to their valuation to move out of these underperforming assets. Don't let these be the only unsavory options facing you when you are in the phase of needing to liquidate holdings to pay for retirement lifestyle expenses.

At the moment, gold is down by a third from its record high in 2011. Even so, the Midas metal has its supporters as a method of preserving value. These advocates have all been riding the down market in hopes of very different results. Only time will tell if holding a sizable amount of gold in one's portfolio is wise or foolish, but one thing that's certain is assets like precious metals don't create any new value or earn any income while waiting for the world's economic story to evolve. Some recommend holding 5-10% of investible assets in precious metals as a form of insurance against a rapidly declining dollar. But even if gold does start to

spike, how do you know the proper timing points to hold and when to sell? And if you are holding this value in numismatic coins, will you be able to find buyers ready to pay the premiums over precious metal content when the market is flashing?

Real estate is moving up out of the recent market correction—in part because the hedge funds and many individual investors are buying rental properties for cash flow as an alternative to traditional financial securities. From 2010-2014 over one-third of all house sales were CASH transactions from investors (in some markets over 50% of sales), which is much higher than in normal market conditions. I interpret this as meaning it's been investor demand that has been propping up the housing market prices because valuations made these purchases more attractive to people seeking alternatives to Wall Street. Can this last? When will the Millennials begin to form households of their own and buy housing…or are they likely to remain apartment and rental house tenants for the long-term? The answer to this question certainly will have an impact on real estate valuations and the attractiveness of owning rental properties.

Without a robust growing economy supported by rising incomes and thriving employment, continued increases in real estate prices are probably doubtful in the near term. There are vastly divergent predictions about overall housing market price trends in 2015 and beyond. Some are advocating that prices will appreciate 5-10%/year, rebounding from pent up demand as our economy thrives. Others have persuasive arguments that suggest prices could deflate 25% or more during the next 10 years as our economy bursts and debt gets reset, driving values back to what they were in the 1970's. Either way, these are massive move predictions in a market sector with historically modest volatility and general inflation.

If you choose to participate in real estate investments, I believe a cautionary tone of not over leveraging one's acquisitions and making sure you buy at below market values would be prudent. But by the same token, don't let pricing volatility dissuade you from prudent opportunities in cash flow rental properties. If you buy it and finance it with conservative assumptions, and control your process, these investment choices can create rivers of passive income over the long run with relatively low risk. If you don't plan to sell the asset in the near term, what does it matter if the price fluctuates yet it continues to cash flow just as you planned?

Planning Implications of Turbulent Times

With all of these confounding trends in all major sectors of our economy, what is a person committed to creating wealth to do with their capital and investment plans? How can they invest it/protect it/grow it in ways they can sleep at night, no matter what happens in the financial markets the day before? How can they be proactive in creating their own personal economy? How can they help their money work harder?

In my opinion, smart money/the sophisticated investor evaluates options outside of the broad financial markets where returns must correlate to the mean performance and market cyclical trends. I propose the prudent individual learn new ways to preserve and build their nest egg, despite the risks of a tumultuous economic environment. Then, if a massive market disruption does occur, perhaps they will be in a position to step in and acquire "deals of a lifetime" from very desperate people. And even if the general market does prosper, holding a strong portfolio of assets that may be appreciating while throwing off cash flow every month, as well, is still a great place to be. In my opinion, focusing on cash flow

investments is a prudent, no-lose path to prosperity. They offer plenty of upside advantage and modest downside risk.

Is Our Government Part of the Problem or Part of the Solution?

When developing our plan and strategies, we must also consider likely impacts of what I consider to be out of control government spending and entitlement obligations. Total US federal debt has increased over 75% in the few short years while Barack Obama has been in office, and government money printing continues to devalue the dollar in real terms. Not that the US is alone in this strategy, all across the globe politicians and central banks are pandering to their populace, spending more each year and digging deep caverns of debt that cannot be rationally seen to ever be paid off. It almost seems like it's become a race to the bottom.

My assessment is not political, just practical. Are the policies driven by Washington DC and the Federal Reserve helping or hurting the majority of people trying to responsibly live their lives and do the right things, or are they being manipulated by the few for personal advantage? Isn't our task of building and preserving wealth hard enough without the government making it more difficult to generate substantial returns in business or investments? Does their confounding maze of regulation or the highest corporate tax rates in the world facilitate the initiation and expansion of new business startups, which create jobs and stimulate the growth of our GDP? Have their trillions of dollars of "stimulus" helped the majority of US citizens' financial well-being or just lined the pockets of Wall Street and the very affluent, connected individuals?

Reported government statistics suggest that inflation is under 2%, and unemployment has fallen under 6% in 2014. Yet many people's gut reaction tells them that these measures have been fabrications relative to the reality experienced by people they know. As our government continues to change how important statistics such as the rate of true inflation or unemployment are calculated, some wonder if they are "cooking the books" for political advantage. I am cautious of believing the feel good news they are preaching.

Our economy is clearly fragile and this so called "economic expansion" has been the most lethargic in the past 90 years. Yes the stock market is flying high, but too many households continue to struggle.

Cogent wealth creation strategies must consider the effects of slow economic growth, as well as the decline of the dollar's purchasing power and the likelihood that taxes will be impacted by the massive government spending spree that has not been adequately funded.

If you view our current economic situation with an unbiased mind, it seems clear this current situation cannot sustain forever, and yet, corrective changes in benefits or taxes could have a devastating effect on many people's financial requirements for retirement. Perhaps the pending 2016 Presidential elections will bring hope of new leaders proposing real solutions. Or if the politicians do nothing and the markets crash, the implications of that scenario may be even more devastating for everyone, regardless of age or financial condition. Either way, those who have been focused on building their own retirement reserves and managing their family budgets will be in the best position to prosper, whatever environment they face.

The main point I am making is *be conservative in your assumptions, and attempt to build a much greater retirement*

reserve or more passive income streams than you think you will need. Don't presume unreasonable planning assumptions in the rate of return your account can achieve. Know the math of what your investments are actually producing. What is the downside if you can be successful in that approach?

Boomers and Millennials

America is undergoing a unique confluence of trends in the economy and demographics during the period from the late 2000's to the late 2020's, which should be factored into your personal financial plan.

In the US, 78 million baby boomers are now in full swing in reaching retirement age, with over 10,000/day moving into their later 60's. This quarter of our population is undergoing dramatic lifestyle changes and will be for the next dozen years. Yet an increasing number of people reaching "retirement age" know they must continue to work to fund basic living expenses because they have not accumulated sufficient savings to fund their ongoing lifestyle expenses as long as they are likely to live.

Government reserves for Social Security and Medicare are not equipped to cover the exploding entitlement obligations as beneficiary roles explode. Nationally, our politicians are bickering like young children, and their only solutions appear to be pointing fingers and kicking the can down the road. The reasonable proposals for fixing our system seem to get ignored. This isn't fair to the beneficiaries who are fearful of the lack of fulfillment or to the younger generations required to pay for this growing obligation in the future.

Unfortunately, it appears that sensible solutions are unlikely to be implemented until the consequences become quite severe, so it is

prudent for each of us, individually, to begin to protect our own well-being with plans and purposeful action before this pending time of economic strife.

If you are one of the few that still enjoy the promise of a defined benefit pension plan that promises to provide income for life, how is your plan's funding doing based on its future obligations? Reports continue to surface describing false assumptions and significant funding shortfalls. While it would be unfortunate if others default on their ability to meet their obligations to you, from your family's standpoint, you will still be responsible for paying your own bills, regardless. Are you prepared with a Plan B solution just in case it is needed?

Traditionally, it has been the younger generation's consumption that is a primary driver of overall economic growth. Is there hope for our current younger generation's financial well-being when many are having difficulty finding meaningful employment at attractive salaries? Add to this the exploding cost of college education generating unprecedented student loan obligations. How can they plan their own lives, yet also accept the folly of the financial burdens placed on them by their irresponsible elders?

Will a slow growth economy and extreme levels of debt be an albatross around the Millennials' necks? Can our young become the huge consumers with family formative expenses, which traditionally have driven our consumption economy?

To be fair to the younger generation, the US needs sound fiscal policies and a growing economy that allows them to prosper. We all should support changes in this direction, even if it causes us a bit of pain today to correct our ship.

The one thing the young have in their favor is time, and with time, as long as one sticks to a reasonable investment plan, long-term

compounding of interest can produce almost magical results. I wish them all the successes in the world; after all, so many people in the older generations are counting on these younger cohorts' contributions to keep our economy afloat and generate future prosperity.

Which Economy Matters?

In this context of possible economic strife, whose financial statements/economy really matters? If you are dependent on government entitlements, you need a solvent government to fulfill those obligations. If you are financially wealthy but all invested in the market, you need a strong US economy with the market valuation stable or growing. If you are invested in sound, private cash flow assets, you should do OK in an up and down economy, provided you are not over leveraged and have protected your downside risk.

Should you have access to liquid capital, there may be opportunities for a huge upside if a crash occurs because there may be the opportunity to buy attractive assets at bargain basement prices, while others are very motivated to sell at any cost. In times of trouble, wealth never disappears; it only gets transferred to those able to pick up the pieces. Now is a perfect time for savvy people to focus on building their intellectual and relationship capital, as well as their financial capital so they are prepared when opportunities emerge.

The point is *your choices and actions decide if you are overwhelmed by your context or if you find ways to leverage this environment to your personal advantage*. I'm a clear proponent of not stressing over a national economy that one can't really influence individually. It is better to *create your own PERSONAL*

ECONOMY that can be doing well despite what is going on nationally. It is better to focus on your personal situation, define and implement a plan that is likely to provide personal advantage within the context of a broad understanding of the environment you are likely to face. Then work this plan diligently.

Opportunities for amazing investments are occurring around you every day. The questions are if you are tuned into them or know people who are, will you will consider taking action, and whether your income statement and balance sheet are aligned to pursue this alternative path? If not today, can it be so tomorrow? It's time to ensure your personal economy is in a strong growth mode.

There Are Positive Perspectives

While many of the prevailing perspectives seem to be negative news of doom and gloom, *we also live in amazing and abundant times.* There are encouraging signs of technological innovation, and America remains the world's incubator of value creation and entrepreneurialism.

Peter Diamandis, author of *Abundance* says "Humanity is now entering a period of radical transformation in which technology has the potential to significantly raise the basic living standards of every man, woman and child on the planet."

Every year, new products and services make people's lives easier, and the select few become very wealthy off of these new businesses. American ingenuity is driving up standards of living all around the world. Concerns about peak energy are seemingly refuted by the exploding supplies of gas and oil driven by technological innovation in drilling. Energy prices are declining, and energy options are expanding—this helps us all. Manufacturing is coming back to America, and prospects for the

future are improving on this front through new technologies like 3D printing.

The developing nations of the world have become providers of so many products at affordable prices; it is truly a win/win situation for raising the living standards of all people across the globe.

Today, anyone with an idea that is valued by others has low barriers of entry to start businesses, particularly online. Our economy is shifting to a service and information economy with little need for the expensive manufacturing infrastructure that was required to build businesses decades ago. Entrepreneurs have access to massive global audiences of customers, and the upside potential of small businesses is truly amazing for those motivated to serve more people.

Our communications are going mobile and small startups that catch the wave of people seeking new ways to capture and utilize information throughout the day, turn small technology companies into billion dollar businesses almost overnight. These devices have amazing capabilities that are being leveraged in new ways every year, if not even quicker. Today, any individual has access to more information than presidents and top advisors had fifty years ago. Tomorrow, our lifestyles will be enhanced through technology that we can't even imagine today. One illustration of this is that, less than a decade ago, smart phones were just a dream in Steve Job's mind. Today, billions of people across the world have access to information and connectivity, which open doors to opportunity because of the ubiquity of these devices. Today change happens at an ever increasing rate.

In the healthcare arena, while we do face challenges on the affordably funding of individual health care coverage, on the innovation front, there are significant advances in almost all areas. There is certainly light at the end of the tunnel toward eradicating

all major diseases and cancers. We are truly living in times of amazing discoveries. When you combine the emerging trends in healthy eating with new medicines and treatment protocols, prospects for increased longevity and vitality are growing every year.

A resurgence of world economic growth could be very beneficial in revenue generation and funding our collective well-being. An individual who is creative and motivated can be a part of the solution and generate wealth through value creation in ways that were unimagined just a few years ago.

As long as you maintain a positive attitude and choose to become a part of the solution, welcome to an epoch of TRUE ABUNDANCE. Those who can imagine a better world will be the ones who help create it. Those who create their own economy can prosper in it.

Which Game Should You Play?

While I enjoyed a successful 30 year career in corporate America in marketing consumer packaged goods products, I was not especially well served by traditional investments/securities or financial advisors that clearly put their interests ahead of mine. Yes, I've experienced great stock market gains on some of the bull markets, but I have also given much of it back through fees and market crashes. At the end of the day, my portfolio did not grow at the rate I expected when I was following the path of Wall Street. I felt that I lacked control and seemed to be simply hoping that luck would provide my financial salvation with big gains.

The old saying is "he who has the gold sets the rules." In my judgment, Wall Street stacks the deck, often in hidden ways. So just like the casinos, no matter what happens, the house always

wins at the expense of the one who is putting up all the money. I have no doubt that the brokers and big financial institutions made out well on my traditional investments over the prior decades—while I took all the risks and received a much smaller portion of the gains than I anticipated, yet absorbed all of the losses. They did not express fiduciary obligation to protect my interests; rather, they set things up for their own personal advantage.

I notice today how about 50% of stock market transactions are these high frequency trading computers talking to other computers creating arbitrage on the slight movements of the markets, holding stocks for less time than it took you to read this sentence. They make these quick moves to suck the profits out of your trade before it is even executed. How can the average investor hope to succeed in a market where the big financial institutions are taking advantage of the smaller investor in this way?

You will see, in a later chapter, how up to $13 trillion of investments are in assets where the basic proposition is you put up 100% of the capital and take 100% of the risk, and yet, if the trade makes money, your financial institution ends up with 60% or more of the upside gain in the long-term—while if you lose money, your broker still gets paid his cut regardless. Who would knowingly agree to such a stacked proposition? Yet nearly 100 million people do.

Now that I have comprehended what was happening, *I've simply chosen to pick up my chips and started play a different game*. In my judgment, there is simply too much to risk to leave my financial future to chance or to let others take advantage of my results. I desire to stack the deck in my family's favor, in ways that are legal and ethical. I am committed to taking bold purposeful action to achieve the financial destination of my choosing.

About 7 years ago, I was laid off from my corporate role as Vice President of Marketing during a time when the world's economy was in a death spiral. Having my family's financial future put into peril, I decided to embark on this path to learn about financial strategies of the wealthy and ways to benefit from non-traditional investments. I believe when you abort constraints of traditional financial planning and mass market investments, you are able to take advantage of privately structured investments for advantage— shifting the odds of success to your favor. I believe this is a forward thinking approach to retirement planning.

It is my understanding that wealth can only be created, never earned. What this means is while mass market investments may be good for compounding at reasonable rates, they take a lifetime to make you "rich" building significant equity. True wealth generation occurs when you create value and participate in opportunities outside of the mainstream—when you learn to serve more people. Business or financial investments that are privately structured can achieve much greater reward yet much less risk and generate a substantial return in a limited time. It's like eating your cake and having it too. Why would you choose to invest in something that isn't structured for your advantage, as long as viable alternatives are possible that are advantaged to you?

Independently structured deals allow the funding partner to control the rules in ways which mitigate risks and magnify returns. In my judgment, this is the only way to gain dramatically higher returns without unreasonable risk and shorten the path to prosperity. So rather than playing a game where all the rules are to the benefit of the big Wall Street institutions, I have discovered the results can be shifted to private advantage when I structure my own deals. And I'm helping others by bringing them into my private deals as partners.

Are There Reliable Investment Solutions?

How should a person navigate these treacherous waters to more securely create wealth during their accumulation years? And how can they preserve their portfolio if traditional markets go through severe declines and tax rates inevitably rise? Are the traditional financial strategies of a diverse portfolio of stocks, mutual funds and bonds tied to the mass market the best bet for your financial future—or are these assets a dangerous inflated bubble ready to pop? Can annuities be the salvation, generating lifetime income streams and protection from market crashes? Or should wise and responsible people turn to private cash flow investments that can be structured in ways that shift the traditional risks and reward paradigm? As you will learn, I have a clear bias to the last two perspectives mentioned.

Depending on your personal age, financial situation, education and desires, there is a unique solution that will best fit your unique situation, and it's up to you to discover it. Your preferred solution may be a combination of a variety of financial strategies and vehicles, but in my opinion, *the "safe" place to put your investment is in areas you know and have a reasonable expectation of control. In deals you fully comprehend how the profits will be made and the risks will be reduced.*

Safe investments are defined by having some modicum of protecting downside risk. Safe investments are relative to your personal knowledge and are, in part, determined by the people you know who bring unique skills and opportunities to the table. In my judgment, if you attempt to become an expert at too many things, you will achieve mastery in none of them. *I believe FOCUS is a key to long-term prosperity and viable risk reduction techniques.*

There is a huge difference between investing and speculation—it comes down to fully comprehending how your money will be

deployed to make a return, while at the same time ensuring the downside risk is addressed. Are you making investment choices because you understand the proposition and risks, or are you wagering on uncertain outcomes? Another term for wagering on uncertain outcomes is gambling.

It seems to me if you can't clearly explain how invested dollars are expected to generate a return and how the downside risk of loss is protected, your investment may really turn out to be a simple gamble. And while it may be fun to bet on the Kentucky derby or go to the casino for a night of excitement, this certainly isn't your best approach when it comes to funding the final trimester of your family's life and their financial security.

I offer a positive perspective and novel approaches to consider. Rather than just blindly following the herd and holding volatile traditional securities, by educating yourself, you can take advantage of lucrative private opportunities to grow cash flow now and build wealth over the long-term in a tax advantaged environment. Investing in privately structured deals may enable the opportunity to shift the risk/reward to your advantage in ways not possible in the broad markets. Inefficient markets create opportunities to buy assets at significant discounts to build your equity even faster. Even if you choose to be a passive investor, why not partner in opportunities where you protect the downside— risk a little and have the opportunity to make a lot? Why not invest in opportunities you can clearly understand?

If you are a believer that America is on the rebound, and we are facing another couple of decades of a bull market, then the stock and bond markets could be a good place to be. While not a pessimist, I am not willing to bet on this outcome. I am concerned the broad financial markets may be bearish during the next decade for the reasons already mentioned. I prefer an alternate path, which can yield the results I'm seeking in a more controlled way—where

what primarily matters is whether the factors of my deal make sense and can I comprehend how it will generate profits regardless of whether the overall economy goes up or down.

In the longer term when you are retired, it may also be advantageous to shift a portion of one's resources into a less risky environment. Specialized annuities can provide a long list of benefits to preserve wealth throughout the remainder of you and your spouse's lives that we will cover in a later chapter.

Choose to Take Action Today

I believe most people who start early enough can build a sustainable retirement portfolio that is sufficient to fund the lifestyle they desire. If you have assets to redirect today, you should be able to achieve your financial foundation in a properly structured portfolio within less than a decade. Even if you find yourself behind the 8 ball today—applying alternative strategies can begin to move you in a positive direction as well—at a much quicker pace than traditional vehicles will ever go.

And for the people who are prepared, the possible pending crisis may represent a phenomenal opportunity to become truly affluent. Wealth is never destroyed—just transferred. For those with capital (financial, relationship or intellectual), sometime during the next decade or so there will likely be unfathomable opportunities to buy desirable assets at pennies on the dollar. But you can only be in the position to prosper if you have the appropriate education, foundational wealth and connections to people able to structure opportunistic deals when the appropriate time comes.

This book is meant to be a call to action. Knowledge is desirable, but wealth is created through implementation. As you will see, as I explain many of the investments I've implemented in my journey

of transformation to Harder Working Money, I certainly am not just dribbling out theory. I have my money in the market in many privately structured deals, and I'm trying to share my insights from real world experience.

Chapter 2—EDUCATIONAL INSIGHTS

This chapter explains many of the financial concepts that led me to pursue the path of Harder Working Money.

The Need for a Plan

An effective plan always begins with the end in mind. Have you figured out what you need to accumulate in retirement reserves or recurring monthly income to be in a position to retire and enjoy the lifestyle you desire? I call your monthly expenses in retirement your *desired lifestyle burn rate*. This budgeted expense not only covers your must-spend money each month, but also those things that are critical for your enjoyment of your life as well. Just be sure that, when projecting your future needs, you are also considering an inflationary factor on spending over the years you are projecting.

Assuming you are currently flowing a traditional approach to retirement planning, do you have a good handle on your current financial situation and the investment glide path that will get you to this destination? What are you reliably able to save/invest each month/year to secure your lifestyle in retirement? What type of rate of return will be required to leverage your current available capital, as well as what you are adding each year in new capital to reach the end point you need to be at in the time available? How are your current investments performing against this benchmark? Answers to these questions are unique to each family's situation, and must be addressed independently. But certainly, lack of clarity in any of these areas will just put your financial destiny up to chance.

Without a well thought through plan, you are unlikely to reach your desired destination.

Whether you are satisfied or fearful of where you stand today, it is only with comprehension of the facts of where you are today that you can begin to build a realistic plan and benchmark your progress.

My interest in wealth building/retirement planning came once I realized my life as a corporate executive was over. For 30 years I was focused on doing well in my career, and our family finances seemed to be taking care of themselves. Then, after 2 ½ years of unsuccessful job search while our national economy was in turmoil, I decided it was time to reinvent myself as an entrepreneur. Much of this book is that story of renewal and transformation.

The Wealth Equation Factors

Achieving wealth and prosperity comes down to simple math and leveraging the proper factors. The fundamental financial reality is that the basic equation of building wealth must always be based on 3 factors: capital, net rate of return (after fees and tax) and time.

Growth of wealth = Capital * Rate * Time

If you are fortunate to start with lots of money, a prudent choice is a game of preservation and safe growth. If you are young and have several decades for accumulation, you can rely upon simple, safe compounding, making automatic contributions and leveraging time. Either of these approaches requires staying the course, having a diversified portfolio and riding through the market cycles. However, if you find yourself in the position similar to the one I'm in—as a 61 year old with limited time before "retirement" and

insufficient capital to rely solely upon "safe market rate of return vehicles" —the only option left is to leverage one's net rate of return. This is the single variable over which we can have substantial control—determined by the types of investments we select and the ways that these deals are structured.

How can we achieve higher net rates of return without putting all our money in risky vehicles and strategies? How can we take full advantage of the loopholes built into our laws directed at incentivizing specific behaviors? How can we rely upon HARDER WORKING MONEY strategies? *The answer I've found is awareness of non-traditional investment options and creatively structuring deals. The answer is leveraging intellectual and relationship capital as much as financial capital.* Sharing these concepts is the purpose of this book.

I've encountered many new mentors with divergent approaches. I've gained insights about distinctive alternative investment strategies from a variety of sources and have been implementing some of these over the past few years with positive results. I am building plans to apply other techniques soon. Other ideas, while interesting, I've decided are not the best solution for my family's needs or current situation. I believe sharing my story will be beneficial for others to understand my insights from this journey.

You may find my experiences interesting, but it is up to you to figure it out what is right for your particular situation and risk profile on your own. Just because something works for others doesn't mean it is right for your situation and personal goals. I only hope that sharing my perspective and experiences will aid in clarifying your situation and options and open your eyes to new investment opportunities that I'm thrilled I've become aware of. I have certainly benefited from the sharing of others and trust that, by paying these insights forward, others will benefit from my experiences.

Foundational Understanding: Rich Dad Poor Dad

When I commenced on this journey of new understanding, I was heavily influenced by Robert Kiyosaki's *Rich Dad Poor Dad* book and then a succession of other books that followed. I've become a big proponent of learning the lessons of private cash flow investing by playing Robert's game, Cash Flow 101. (It is far better to learn one's lessons of evaluating investments and the accounting rules of income statements and balance sheets on paper before you take action in the real world). At any rate, my journey to developing the concept of Harder Working Money is the culmination of trying to apply many of Robert's foundational principles:

- Get a financial education so you can take personal control of your financial destiny, mirroring how the wealthy utilize their income statements and balance sheets to create sustainable prosperity.
- Become active in the Business and Investor side of the cash flow quadrant, learning to take advantage of incentivized benefits in structuring to reduce taxes and keep more of what you earn, rather than just being an Employee or Self-employed professional trading time for money and paying the highest tax rates.
- The long-term game is to transition savings from one's active income into building a portfolio of cash flowing assets, so these passive income assets provide the lifetime benefit of paying for one's desired lifestyle expenses, now and through retirement.
- Learn to think like a wealthy person focused on increasing cash flow through efficiency and using positive leverage to maximize returns.
- Learn to leverage intellectual capital and relationship capital more than one's personal financial capital and build an ever-scalable business of privately structured deals.

- Understand that risk is really just being out of control, not understanding how money will make money in a proposition/just speculating that an asset's value will go up, while control implies understanding the deal specifics and controlling downside risk through proper structuring and risk mitigation.

What became clear to me is that people who are employed and trying to win the prosperity game through modest savings using traditional financial assets are in for a very long-term game. This is a game that many people can never win given their current earning/spending habits and remaining time available. If the requirement to possibly maintain one's lifestyle into one's late 80's or 90's means amassing 1-3 million dollars, it will take several decades of consistent contributions and growth. And it also requires luck that the markets don't crash when you are nearing retirement without decades to rebound.

On the other hand, if you are actively putting together privately structured deals, and you control a great one, you can literally control tens or hundreds of thousands of dollars within a month. *Great deals are magnetic to money*. Certainly, the funding won't be all yours, but you can structure things so you are creating arbitrage on other people's money (spreads where the investment earns more than the cost of funds) and personally benefitting for using your knowledge and relationships as an intermediary with the skills to put the deals together.

Robert teaches that there are two types of investors. Active investors have the knowledge and relationships to find and put together privately structured opportunities for specific advantage. Passive investors either just play an uninformed game from the sidelines hoping their plans work out—or they can choose to leverage the relationships with other active investors to get involved in privately structured deals offering private participation.

Either way, passive investors are seeking returns on their money, while active investors are seeking unique opportunities to create leverage and control, often with money that isn't fully theirs. Clearly, the role of an active investor is the game I'm now trying to master, and as such the insights from this journey are the ones I am sharing with you. Once I get my future prosperity secure, I look forward to transitioning more to the passive investor role.

Private deals have become a real game changer in my planning and investing. Completing a continuous flow of deals becomes a clear pathway to my objectives. This approach feels very compelling as a quicker way to get my financial house in order to sustain our lifestyle for decades to come.

Earn More Than You Spend & Invest the Difference

One obvious basic principle of wealth building starts with the fact that you must control your spending to save/invest something for the future. This can be achieved with a blending of three factors. If you earn more, you obviously have the opportunity to save more. But the amount you earn isn't necessarily controllable in the short-term. Discretion comes in how much you choose to spend and what you choose to set aside in your savings/investing account. Then, once investing, the greatest impact can often come in how you structure your personal financial wealth creation engine. In other words, what is the allocation of the investment classes that you choose to distribute your investable money into?

People who have chosen to live beyond their means on credit are creating high hurdles to overcome in their long-term prosperity plan. If you are serious about achieving prosperity in the future, this behavior must be addressed now. Work out a budget. Figure out how you can earn more. Control your desire for instant

gratification. Learn to pay yourself first by automatically putting the first dollars you earn into your investment account, and create a budget to live joyfully on what is left over. If you are fortunate enough to get a raise or have an investment payout, consider how much of this gain can be directed to your investment portfolio for the long-term, rather than just spending the new windfall today.

One consideration about debt that most people do not recognize is that it is not just the added cost of interest that disadvantages your long-term wealth building...*you also must consider the opportunity cost of what you could have done with the money spent on interest instead, and how this could have compounded over the long-term.*

Consider an example that you are driving a 4 year old car with 75,000 miles on it. You are thinking about buying a new car. On the one hand, you are about to make your final car payment on your current vehicle, and for an out-of-pocket cost of $6,000, you can trade in this car and pick up a new one with monthly payments similar to the ones you have now. So at first glance, you think getting the new car will cost you $6,000. On the other hand, if you wait a couple of years, driving your existing car to 100,000 miles, you would end up with two years of no car payments, a savings of approximately $7,200. Perhaps, at that time, your cost to drive away in a new car with the same payments would now be $7000. So, by waiting for the new car the extra two years, you would net savings of $6,200. If you simply invested the $6,200 savings (from not paying car payments for two years) and held it in an 8% return tax advantaged account, over the next 25 years this one-time decision to delay buying a new car could net you $42,460. That is more than the price of a car without payments, just based on the decision to delay the purchase and invest instead!

I use this as a simple example of demonstrating the long-term consequences of the choices we make. *Learning to maximize*

benefits of the cash that flows through our lives can pay long-term dividends toward prosperity. It's not all about denial and savings. It's also about properly investing what we do save in ways that earn a decent return. Through proper planning, we may be able to discover how to legitimately structure to pay lower (or at least delay) taxes, how we can minimize fees and how we can shelter passive income flows. *When we learn to stack multiple benefits, it can dramatically increase long-term gains*. After all, it's not just what we make, but what we keep for personal investment and consumption that matters.

Taxes Are The #1 Hurdle of Wealth Building

Do you realize that your number one expense in life is taxes? Adding up federal & state income taxes, property taxes and other local taxes you pay such as sales tax added to all purchases and the $.30-.70/gallon tax you pay on gasoline really take a huge bite out of your income/cash flow. Even low earning people who don't pay federal income tax can easily spend 25% of all of their gross cash flow on taxes, while the rest of us generally pay 50% or more. As previously illustrated, the greater your after tax net-income is, the more you have the choice to save and invest. I certainly don't support any trickery to avoid one's fair share of funding our government, but I am a proponent of *playing the game within the rules as they have defined them, being as tax efficient as possible*. Money that you save in taxes can not only improve your lifestyle today; if invested, this savings can accelerate your investment results.

When it comes to your ability to save/invest—and then pay taxes on the growth of your savings—the rate of tax you pay on your investments significantly impacts your ability to compound over the long run and achieve your prosperity goals. Reducing, or at

least delaying, taxes can greatly affect your ability to build significantly greater wealth in a shorter period of time. Realize that different income is taxed at different rates. And if you personally own a small business, there can be significant positive tax ramifications from this as well.

The following illustration is clearly not a real scenario, but it does exemplify the point of the big bite taxes can take from your ability to compound an investment portfolio over time.

If you start with $1.00 and double it every year for twenty years, ($2.00, $4.00, $8.00, etc.) by the 20th doubling, it will amount to $1,048,576! However, if each year the gain is taxed at only 15%, (so the net growth becomes $1.85, $3.42, $6.33 etc.) by the 20th doubling, it will amount to only $220,513. So taking out 15% of the growth each year reduces the cumulative total by 79%. Wow…what a big bite taxes take out of our ability to grow our investments.

At a 20% tax rate the total only grows to $127,482; at 28% to $51,353; at 33% to $28,466 and at 39% tax to only $13,693. How can that be? You reduce the growth each year by 39%, and you eliminate over 98% of the possible gain! Such is the power of compounding. It can work for you, or it can work against you as we have demonstrated in both taxes and fees.

This example of the impact of taxes on your ability to grow your money is a very clear demonstration of the benefits of placing your retirement portfolio in a traditional IRA/401K— and especially the dramatic difference it can make if you establish/convert to a Roth account, which compounds and allows you to reap the long-term benefits tax free. When you are in your prime earning years, *failure to set aside sufficient current income in a tax advantaged way can be a major impediment to maximizing your long-term retirement account accumulation*.

Few take the time to plan and be proactive to minimize the effect of taxes on their financial/retirement planning. But now that you understand the devastating impact on your ability to grow your portfolio to the levels needed to fund your desired lifestyle burn rate, you should clearly comprehend the benefit of tax efficiency, including structuring deals so your growth is taxed at a capital gains rate rather than at a regular income rate.

Review your situation with your tax advisor; have them help you pursue a path that maximizes your opportunity to accumulate wealth. ***Beneficial tax opportunities are one prime reason I'm drawn to real estate as a key part of my Harder Working Money plan,*** because real estate provides a number of tax advantages not available with other investment classes.

A Coffee Today or Forty Seven Large in Two Decades? The Power of Compounding

Many of our routine life expenses seem so trivial. Whether it's going out to eat or just having a Starbucks coffee every day. But over time, these small expenses really add up, not just in the out-of-pocket expense, but more significantly, in the opportunity cost of what the money could have earned over time if prudently invested and left to compound.

If you started saving only $20 a week from your current spending and invested it in a tax advantaged account at 8% net return, do you realize this $1040/year investment would cumulate and compound to $47,592 in the next 20 years. More than double your input. Small changes in behavior can have a big impact over time!

Compounding really magnifies the effect of small sacrifices for delayed gratification today, for long-term benefit through

investing. An important element is automating this contribution so it regularly goes into your investment account. If you choose to not go out to dinner tonight for added savings, but leave the cash in your checking account, before long it will probably end up being spent on something else. It's *only when you set up a routine savings and investment plan that your positive choices can cumulate into significant long-term benefit*.

Just to carry the analogy a bit further, keep up this $20/week investment practice for a 3rd decade, and it would total $117,815. By the 4th decade, it would grow to almost $270,000! Such is the dramatic power of compounding. By the 40th year, you would have deposited $41,600 into your account, but because of the power of compounding, it would be worth over 6 ½ times more. You would have gained $227,818 just with the decision to set a small amount weekly in a well thought through investment, consistently keep the weekly deposit and never interrupt the compounding with early withdrawals.

I'm certainly not suggesting that one not enjoy life's little pleasures. I'm just suggesting you realize the long-term impact of your choices in what you elect to spend versus invest today. Once you have figured out your family's current budget and retirement funding plan and are automatically saving/investing what your plan calls for, certainly you should pursue things that add enjoyment in life on some of the extra funds left over. In fact, as we'll discuss below, you need to plan for setting aside some money into your just for me/fun account when budgeting.

Since small investments can have such a dramatic impact over the long run, it demonstrates that the power of compounding can work for everyone. This example clearly demonstrates that it is within the reach of everyone to fund significant contributions toward their retirement if they simply have the will and consistency to do it, and start down this path early enough.

If just $20 a week can have this significant result, why not invest much more for quicker attainment of your goals? Traditional financial advisors have recommended that if you start early, a reasonable plan would be to save a minimum of 10% of your total income. So if across your earning years, you averaged making $50,000, it would equate to $5,000/year or $96/week. If your combined family income averaged $100,000/year, it would equate to $192/week. Just think; these are almost 5 and 10 times the amount in the example above. So in 20 years you could cumulate $238,000 or $476,000 (for $96 or $192/week), in 30 years $589,000 or $1,178,000 or in 40 years $1,347,000 or $2,694,000! Yes, if you start early enough and stick to it through thick and thin, and you learn how to structure your investment account for realistic/consistent returns, your retirement requirements should be definitely achievable.

The theory works great, *but what if you don't have 30-40 years left to cumulate these big account balances*? That is what the remainder of this book tries to address, but one key answer is to focus on improving one's net rate of return, without also increasing risk.

The Compounding Growth Curve: Compounding Is a Long-Term Game

As previously explained, it is critical to comprehend that compounding moderate rate interest growth is a very long-term proposition. Compounding growth is exponential. This means you accumulate small gains at first, but once you are earning interest on top of interest on top of interest, the annual gains can become quite significant in distant years.

This is one reason financial advisors trying to sell you something like to show you cash accumulation tables over 25 or 30 years. If they simply showed what would occur in the next 2-3 years, you might not get as excited at the results, since they are so slow to build. (For example, in the $20/week at 8% net return example illustrated previously, at the end of year 3, you would have contributed $3060, and your account would be worth $3,376 for a 10% gain of $316—quite a perceptual difference than saying in 30 years it's worth almost $118,000 on a contribution of $31,200 for a 270% gain of $86,614. But it's all with the same math, just at different points on the compounding curve.)

It is important to realize that the earlier you start and more consistently you contribute and compound → the quicker you will get to the point where accumulation is substantial. A critical element is to not interrupt the build up with hiatuses in contributions, cyclical market losses or untimely disbursements.

A corollary example we all are likely to understand may be helpful. When it comes to the power of compounding interest, it can work for you or against you depending on whether you are paying or receiving the interest.

Many of us who have purchased homes have faced the issue of deciding if it is prudent to refinance our loans when interest rates go down a little bit. One of the keys in this decision is how long you have been paying down your mortgage versus how much the new monthly payment savings would be.

Most people comprehend that the way loan amortization works is that, during the first several years, you pay lots of interest and very little principle reduction. Then the situation changes over time.

For example, let's assume you borrowed $200,000.00 at 5% interest on a 30 year amortizing loan. Your monthly payment

(principal and interest) would be $1,073.64/month. So in the first year, you would have made total payments of $12,883.68; however, your principal balance owed would still be $197,049.27. That means only $2,950.73 (23%) went to principal reduction and 77% went to interest. No wonder there are so many happy bankers.

On the other hand, when you get to the last year of payoff, you are still paying $1,073.64/month, but 97% of your payment is going to principal reduction and only 3% to interest. No wonder the banks like to entice people to refinance their mortgages whenever possible to keep restarting at the beginning of the amortization curve.

Similarly, this principle works to your benefit in accumulating investment values over the long-term. In a sense, when investing, you are playing the role of the bank. You are getting the benefits of compounding effects over time. The longer your money has to work to achieve the result you desire, the less the rate of return needs to be to achieve the result you are seeking. Like so many exponential growth graphs, compounding returns are in the so called hockey stick shape. There are small perceived gains at first when interest is just working on the initial principal contribution; however, in the long-term, when interest is compounding on top of lots of interest, you get huge gains each subsequent year.

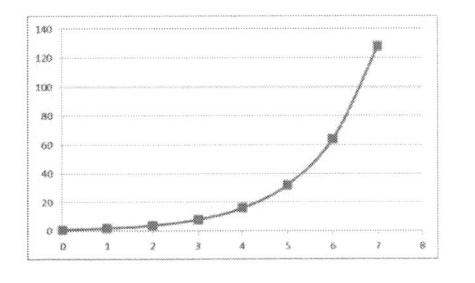

Compounding Growth Curve

The implication of this lengthy period of modest growth then reaching the critical inflection point when growth becomes exponential in the long-term is to realize compounding returns is a long-term game. It's simple math and always works if you follow the rules. However, for this plan to work out, you must get started early and stick to the plan without fail. Disruption to the growth curve means that you will accrue only a small portion of the gain (from the front part of the graph) and miss out on the big gains (at the back part of the graph). Just like resetting your mortgage rate and slipping back to the top of the amortization table, if you take out distributions or if you experience massive market losses, this program takes a huge step backwards. The time to the exponential growth phase just keeps moving further and further away, while you are moving closer and closer to the time you need to start taking distributions for retirement.

The Impact of Rate of Return and NET Rate of Return

When investing, it's obvious that the average rate of return that money earns has an impact on the time it takes money to grow. However, many don't realize the scale of impact a few percentage points can make.

The following table represents the time in years it takes for capital to double just on the compounding interest (no new capital invested each year, also no withdrawals/taxes).

Interest Rate	Years to Double
2%	36 years
4%	18 years
6%	12 years
8%	9 years
10%	7.2 years
12%	6 years
14%	5.2 years
16%	4.5 years
18%	4 years
20%	3.6 years
22%	3.3 years

You may have heard the term the rule of 72, which says if you divide 72 by an interest rate, it will tell you how long in years it will take to double. So in an extreme example, if you wanted to double your money in only two years, it would require finding an investment earning 36% interest. On the other hand, if you put your money in something very safe, like a US Treasury Note that is currently paying only about 2%, it would take 36 years to double in value.

What is obvious by studying the chart is that *at lower interest rates, a small difference in rate can have a very dramatic difference in time,* but at higher rates, a couple of points difference don't make all that much difference in the time to double. Keep this in mind if you are considering "safe" 2-4% returns versus choosing different options that can yield double or triple that rate of return in a risk controlled manner.

What is NET RATE OF RETURN, and why is it so important? There are two key factors in investing that can dramatically impact your net results: fees and taxes.

Let's say you are considering investing on a hot tip by your broker in a mutual fund that he says has averaged 8% return over the past year. Of course, he is typically quoting the gross return of the fund when he is describing the performance of the fund, leading you to believe this is what you will receive. Think again. As described other places in this book, on average, the combined (often hidden) costs of a mutual fund average 3.1%/year. So while the fund may report 8%, your net effective growth is compounding at 4.9%. So instead of your money doubling in 9 years, it would double in 14.7 years.

If this investment was not made in a tax advantaged environment (in your investment portfolio outside of an IRA/401K), you would also be paying taxes each year on the interest earned. Because this is a managed fund where the underlying stocks are constantly being purchased and sold to try to chase yield, gains will end up being taxed as earned income, rather than capital gains. Let's call the likely applicable tax rate 33%. So the net effect is that your capital does not compound at 4.9%, but at 3.28%. Of course this means that now, as you watch your account try to grow, you see it will only double in 22 years.

In other words, instead of doubling in 9 years as you expected, you may need to wait 2.4 times longer for your account to double because of fees and taxes. An attractive investment option has turned out to be not so attractive. No wonder people look at their investment portfolio accounts, hear the markets are doing well but wonder why their account balances don't seem to grow very fast.

If you don't have a long time until retirement and need to see your retirement account grow rapidly, *it is critical that you become an expert in investment EFFICIENCY*. How can you participate in opportunities that generate a desirable gross rate of return and are also in a tax advantaged environment and where fees are minimized for an effective net rate of return? This is one reason

why *I am drawn to privately structured investment opportunities—where you have greater control on the parameters of the investment to maximize personal benefit and are not suspect to hidden fees*.

Understanding Investment Risk vs. Reward

On multiple occasions I've mentioned shifting the risk/reward paradigm. It is *essential that you fully comprehend this strategy if you desire to accomplish more in a shorter period of time,* if you want to achieve Harder Working Money.

There are two aspects you must understand about any investment to be in a position of fully evaluating how appealing it might be and how applicable it may be to help you progress in your investment plan: risk and reward.

The first aspect of any investment is **REWARD**. The obvious element of this is the rate of return on the investment. Some investments provide a stated return. If you buy a bond or annuity that promises to pay 4% interest, or you make a private loan for 10% interest, you are certain that you will get that return—short of a default. Other investments provide an expected rate of return. You may think you are to receive 8% cash on cash return if you own rental real estate (provided there are not excessive expenses or vacancies), or you may expect that a company dividend on a stock you hold will generate 5% return (because this is what it has been historically); however, you must wait until the payout to see what you really receive versus the expected rates of return.

Other assets don't generate any immediate cash flow/return. You buy them simply hoping they will appreciate to generate your reward over time. If you buy a stock that doesn't pay a dividend, or if you buy a precious metal such as gold, your total "paper" return

will be calculated based on the price you paid for it versus today's value.

You purchase these types of assets because you believe/speculate the value will go higher in the future. For example, if you purchased a stock for $50 last year, and today it is worth $55, theoretically you have made 10% return on your money. I say paper return and theoretically because it could be worth more or less tomorrow; you haven't really captured any true return until you sell the asset. Your basis remains what you paid for the asset. However, I will say having seen my previous 401K balances go up and up as the stock market rose in the 80's and 90's and then come crashing back down, I certainly felt that the losses were real because emotionally I'd already emotionally banked the gains.

The second aspect to understand in any investment is **RISK**. This term relates to how certain the anticipated outcome is to occur or what other possible outcomes may occur. There are two related aspects of certainty of outcome: volatility and likelihood of a specific outcome.

When you hear the term volatility, this is a statistical term that relates to the amount of variability in the result versus the mean. Let's say you expected 8% return, and over time, it varied between 7% and 9%. This is a low volatility, low risk situation because no matter the specific outcome you are very likely to get close to what you desire. On the other hand, if you expected 8% return, and over time, it varied between -4% and +20%, this is a high volatility, high risk result. Sometimes you may be very pleasantly surprised, while other times you could be very frustrated with the outcome. From a math standpoint, the average return is the same between these two examples, but from an investment and security standpoint, these are very different investments and involve very different levels of risk because of the volatility.

The second aspect is likelihood or predictability of outcome. I view this more as a measurement of speculation; however, it can certainly be an element of intelligently understanding an investment sector if you fully comprehend the likely outcomes.

Let's say you have the opportunity to make an investment where, for every $1.00 you invest, there is a 50% chance that you will lose all your money, a 25% chance you will neither win nor lose any money and a 25% chance you will "win." Is this an investment you would consider buying?

At first glance, it seems like a bad deal with lots of downside risk and only a minimal chance of upside. However, a key element of the investment you need to understand before you can judge if it is appealing is the magnitude of the "win" in the small chance you do get that result. Let's say in that case you could get back $10-20.00 for every dollar invested in the 25% of the time you win.

Now you can see this situation is similar to a roulette table in a casino, yet the odds are stacked in your favor rather than in the favor of the house. In the long run, you don't need good luck to win, just enough spins of the wheel. Is this scenario really a bad bet? Probably not, depending on how many dollars you have to work with, how much time is available to achieve your desired outcome and your personal tolerance for risk. Is it the type of investment opportunity I'm currently looking for? Not at this time. I'm looking for more predictable results in my investments, more consistent returns and less chance of losing my principal.

These probabilities of low likelihood outcomes might be in business startups or new product launches or companies with speculative businesses like new prescription drugs. It's a risky game; you must realize that there will be many times you will lose money, so you need to have deep pockets, and you don't want to invest too much into any one deal. And you must have sufficient

time for the big win to come your way. However, if there is certainty that some outcomes will be very big wins for you—as long you keep playing long enough—you are also certain to come out a big-time winner over time.

This scenario is the analogy to how a lottery works. Lotteries love to pay out the big jackpots because they attract lots of players, and yet, the lottery company is able control the math in the structure of the payouts in a way that they are certain to retain big profits. They know with the billons of tickets that are purchased, they can attract people hoping to be one of the few winners, and yet, most people lose a small amount.

My overall perspective on risk asks the questions: *How much can one know about the range of volatility and how much control can one have on the certainty of outcomes?* If you have control of factors in a deal, such as the ability to manage the risk factors in a mortgage as a private lender or the way an annuity is structured for your specific benefit, the investment can be structured or controlled for minimal risk.

Knowledge + Control = Less Risk

On the other hand, if you just check a box on a 401K form at work, and really know nothing about the underlying market sectors or why the mutual funds you are participating in should generate a positive return or the fees you are paying, in my opinion, you are participating in a higher risk scenario. Unfortunately, this describes how most people are investing today.

Warren Buffet is not a believer in the traditional allocation strategy of a diversified portfolio of stocks/bonds/mutual funds across a variety of market sectors to limit risk. He said *"Wide diversification is only required when investors do not understand what they are doing."* I find this point of view compelling. While I

do believe you are prudent to protect your downside when concentrated in a single investment sector—the more I can know about how my money will be used to make money, the more familiar I am with the factors controlling the riskiness of the deal—the more certain I can be that a given investment is either right or wrong for me.

Typical Market Based Risk & Reward Pricing

The big financial Wall Street markets tend to price the risk one is willing to take into the reward likely to occur. This happens naturally as a function of supply and demand in the allocation of capital. If the perceived reward is greater than the related risk, more money will flow into that market until the pricing advantage is neutralized. ***Efficient markets like balanced risk and reward.***

For example, consider these different assets' risks and returns on two scales, each 1-10, with 1 being no risk/very low reward and 10 being very high risk/high potential for reward:

- Treasury bonds are probably the least risky investment class there is. They are backed by the full faith and credit of the United States government, because whether or not your bond has any value. The government has the ability to print the money to pay you back. As such, bonds are a 1 on the risk scale (very low risk). However, today you also earn only a very modest rate of return, 2% or so, and this is below the real rate of inflation. So I consider these a loser's bet. Yes, you are certain you will get your 2% return without fail, but the purchasing power of your money is also going down while you wait to be repaid. So in reality, it is a certain loss. Perhaps the only reason this would be a good investment to make is that if all other assets were

crashing, this could be perceived to be a storehouse of some value, so your money is not losing more in something else.

- Typical big company stocks, which pay dividends, are normally low risk/low reward assets to own. For example, I worked for General Mills, Sara Lee and ConAgra for over 20 years and owned a significant amount of stock in each of these companies at one point in my life. I would consider them to be 2-3 on the risk scale (because they are big consumer packaged goods companies with strong brands, the certainty of their cash flow pay out reliable dividends). Over time, they also generated reasonable returns of 5-6% in dividend payments plus appreciation in stock values, so I'd characterize them as 2-3 on the reward scale as well.

- High growth/highly volatile stocks come in slightly above the middle of the scales of risk and reward. Consider Apple Computer as an example of the middle risk and reward type of investment. In many instances over the last 10 years with the introduction of massive new products like the iPhone or the iPad, the tremendous growth in sales has often caused Apple's stock price to double. But by the same token, Apple's stock price has also plummeted with competitive market introductions and litigation versus Samsung over trade infringement issues. Since there is a chance that, over a short period of time, the stock could go way up in value or way down in value, it is probably a 5-6 on the risk scale and also a 5-6 on the reward scale. It is simply a very volatile stock. And while it is one of the strongest brands worldwide, given a high current price to earnings ratio, there is a reasonable chance that next year's value may not support sustaining the same stock price it is today. So if I were to consider investing in a stock like this, I'd be learning a lot about the exciting news of upcoming product

launches, but I'd always have a stop loss in place to protect the downside.

- Finally there are truly speculative ventures: an offering on an unproven business or a company that does exploratory drilling for oil wells or a drug company trying to find the next wonder drug. Each of these has high risk of failure (9-10 on the risk scale), but also huge potential upside in the long run (9-10 on the reward scale). The appeal of these investment opportunities is the potential to strike it rich with the ones that hit, perhaps earning 10-50 times your amount invested over the initial 5 years or so. So investors in these types of ventures don't mind the strikeouts, they just keep searching for the next homerun.

What you will notice in all of these examples is that the risk/reward tends to be correlated. That is a function of an efficient market deploying capital systematically.

Asymmetrical Risk & Reward in an Inefficient Market

In my opinion what *the savvy investor should always be looking for is stacking the deck in their own favor*. In these situations a higher than typical reward is possible, and yet, risks can be reduced. (When you are able to achieve much higher rewards than risk, this relationship is described as asymmetrical.)

For example, at the moment I have a private mortgage extended to a person who rehabs and flips single family homes that will generate over12% return on capital to the funders. And yet, we have only lent 62% loan to the value of the improved property. With a huge cushion of protective equity, there is virtually no risk to our money. Could things go wrong and perhaps take a while for

us to claim the property in a default? Yes, but with so much downside protection we would have plenty of room to claim and sell the property while still earning a desirable rate of return on our funds. It is the borrower who is in the risky position. By choosing to take the role of the bank and only making safe loans, we set ourselves up for a very desirable asymmetrical risk and reward. I would characterize this as a 2-3 on the risk scale and a 5-6 on the reward scale.

In my opinion, utilizing *private structuring of deals is a way that allows the individual investor to win in the game of shifting risk and return and more quickly attain financial freedom*. These types of deals are only possible in inefficient markets that cannot attract big capital; they are uniquely structured investment opportunities out of the mainstream. They are unique one off deals that you are fortunate to encounter. These are deals that the big players cannot take over and manipulate the game to their advantage because of scale. These are opportunities to structure deals, which provide the opportunity for bigger returns and yet not incur more risk.

To further explain the advantage to the individual versus Wall Street, let's consider an example of buying a single family investment property versus buying stock in a big financial company controlling lots of real estate, a Real Estate Investment Trust.

Big money needs scale. If you are a REIT seeking consistent cash flow in real estate, you are likely to be looking to build a portfolio of "trophy" assets worth $20-50 million each or even much more. It's certainly more efficient to acquire and run a larger complex of properties than one where the average asset value is only $2-5 million. If you are a business trying to deploy $200 million in the next couple of years, it's a question of a building portfolio of 5-8 assets versus 50-80. And you certainly are not interested in

attempting to place the same money going into 1,500 single family homes. What a management headache.

Because of the mass of money on Wall Street chasing these deals, there is huge competition amongst the big players for the available, desired larger assets (limited supply and lots of demand). Hence, the prices get bid up/expected returns come down. Typical returns on capital for class A trophy commercial real estate tend to run about 4-5% CAP rate, generating slightly higher cash on cash return when funded with attractive long-term financing. They are great for consistent expected results (low risk), but also relatively low expected returns (low reward). Furthermore, with high demand, these trophy assets rarely are sold at a significant discount to full market value. The only opportunity for gains is based on the long-term cash flow and protecting money against the devastating effect of loss of purchasing power. Efficient markets generate nice, safe returns on great properties but modest returns, symmetrical risk/rewards.

At the other end of the scale, are the inefficient markets of an investor buying single family homes to turn into rentals. At any given point there are tens of thousands of properties nationwide that could be available for this purpose, each in a different location and a different state of repair, each with pros and cons as potential rental properties. A select few are available by "motivated sellers" and could be purchased far under fair market value; others can only be purchased at top dollar. While at the same time, there are thousands of possible buyers; however, each buyer wants a different location and has a different ability to get funding and take down the deal. Most investors are only aware of and considering a very small number of properties before they buy. So you would characterize this market as high supply and low demand. *Inefficient markets are rife with opportunity for investors that*

***know how to ferret out great deals and know how to properly
structure deals.***

In general, an average rental property can generate cash on cash
returns of 8%+ on a good deal that is properly structured on the
initial buy. This rate of return is higher than the commercial deals
mentioned above since every house is different and the big money
isn't chasing all these little deals. With less demand, there is more
opportunity on the buyer's side than seller's side in negotiating.
Good deals are one off opportunities that get properly structured
for personal advantage. Furthermore, it is very often the case that
on the purchase of investment properties they will be acquired at a
discount to the true market value (high supply/low demand), so
there is the opportunity to generate significant equity as well as
more desirable cash flow.

Welcome to the wonders of inefficient markets and the ability to
privately structure advantageous deals. But by the same token, ***in
inefficient markets investors must be wary because not all deals
are good deals***. You must bring specific knowledge to ferret out
the good ones...or you must partner with people who have that
capability.

So a key differentiator in this type of investing is on the risk side of
the equation. How much intellectual and relationship capital is the
investor bringing to the party...can they find the great deals?
Significant gains of equity in real estate are made on the buy. If
one has an inside track and can acquire a property at a 15-30%
discount to the potential value of an asset, because an experienced
real estate investor knows how to spot value and correct small
problems, the net long-term return can safely be double the
average cash on cash return. This is the appeal I'm seeking in real
estate. The long-term possibility of double digit compounding of
returns plus other tax benefits too.

The point I'm attempting to make is that it's only in inefficient markets that the savvy investor can shift the advantage to their side of the equation. By learning new skills and structuring private deals, it is possible to establish opportunities with 2X, 5X or even 10X returns versus conservative Wall Street investment opportunities, without all the costly fees.

Even if you don't know how to locate and structure these deals yourself, *there are plenty of opportunities to get money invested in these investment opportunities by partnering with people who have access to lots of great deals but need more capital to take advantage of them all*. Welcome to the world of joint venturing on privately structured deals. This has been the mainstay of how the affluent accumulate and preserve wealth for generations. Now it is something that is becoming more prevalent to the investor seeking yield but looking outside of the volatile Wall Street markets. Money that gets applied to high reward/low risk deals becomes Harder Working Money.

Summary Thoughts on Risk

My overall perspective on risk assessment it's not how much you win or lose on any given deal that matters, but across deals how much money you make when you are right vs. how much money you lose when you are wrong…and the frequency of these outcomes. Whether you are in Wall Street securities or privately structured deals, there will always be losing trades/deals. But it is how you manage your risk that matters as well as what the overall returns during a year are. Never bet all of your money in one trade, rather figure out an allocation strategy and have a maximum exposure to any single deal. Always put stops in if you buy risky stocks to protect the downside and limit losses. Always make secured loans with a large cushion of protective equity if you make

private loans. Always start with substantial positive equity on the buy if you purchase a property. With these and other mitigating strategies, *you can limit the downside when things go against you and your overall portfolio should have attractive returns in total*.

Should I Consider Paying Off My Mortgage?

One of the biggest sources of equity that most successful people have is their private residence. I've often been asked by people what I think are the advantages of early payoff versus maintaining a 30 year fixed rate mortgage on my home.

I believe that keeping a mortgage on your personal residence is prudent for several reasons:

- Interest rates are so attractive today…if they go up in the future I win by having maintaining a low fixed rate mortgage, if they go down significantly I can always refinance to move to the lower level. In either way I am leveraging other people's money at less than 5% cost of funds over the long-term. I can make many times this with my capital in other investments.
  - The interest you pay is also a beneficial tax deduction
- In the long-term if the dollar continues to devalue…having a substantial mortgage balance is like shorting the dollar because it allows me to pay off long-term debt with lower value currency
  - This point shouldn't be lost on Rental properties as well. I love accumulating long-term "good debt" on cash flow properties. Over time as my rents go up and the value of the dollar goes down, I'm paying back the bank with cheaper dollars.

- We live in a litigious society. If you are at fault in an accident, the 1st thing a lawyer will do to try to see your net worth is to see if you have substantial equity in your personal residence. Owning a free and clear home can become a magnet for lawsuits.
- There is a sophisticated strategy to accelerate the payoff of a mortgage without increasing my out of pocket expense that I'm looking into, however, even if I pursue this approach as soon as my mortgage gets paid off I'll then re-leverage my house with a new mortgage.
    - o This way I'll maintain my tax deduction for interest expense reducing my tax liability
    - o I'll have a new source of capital to use in higher return investments.

Overall, I intend to keep my personal residence mortgaged to a reasonable degree (maintaining at least 25% equity even after the possibility of adding a HELOC). However, I'm also of the firm belief that people who simply desire to own their home free and clear are making a poor choice financially. Perhaps it reduces stress to live without debt. However, having a lot of equity on your balance sheet that isn't income producing may represent a missed opportunity. It may the biggest tool in your toolbox that could help you build financial freedom, but most people are not using it so.

Chapter 3—BUILDING A TRADITIONAL FINANCIAL PLAN

Regardless of the retirement planning strategy that you choose to pursue, you need a financial plan as a roadmap to clarify where you are today and the appropriate route that can get you to your desired destination.

Buckets and Financial Planning

When most planners discuss a financial plan, they typically use an analogy of dividing your income into multiple buckets. Since the first thing that happens to your money is paying current expenses, I like to visualize it as pouring all the income in to one bucket and the excess overflowing into others.

A family's after tax net income is like water pouring into the top bucket: the *SPENDING* bucket. The spending bucket has holes in it, releasing money with every expense so it must be constantly refilled. If you tend to be credit oriented and often spend more than you earn, the spending bucket never fills up. You make up the overspending by putting expenses on credit cards, which will need to be paid from future income flowing into your bucket plus interest. So this really just adds more holes to the spending bucket, compounding your financial difficulties.

Of course the ideal situation is to earn more, as well as budget and constrain spending, so this expense bucket overflows every month and the excess is captured by other buckets for specific purposes. If you get a raise, or if you add additional passive income streams,

filling the spending bucket and not correspondingly increasing spending, more will overflow. That is the objective we should all be after: capturing the cascading waterfall's overflow in order to build a prosperous future, turning the excess cash flow of our lives into Harder Working Money.

The middle bucket is often called the **SAVINGS** bucket. This includes the liquid cash you set aside for future intended expenses and emergencies. It is prudent to keep it always full (at your predetermined plan level). This bucket is a safety net. It provides security if, for some reason, your income is halted for a period (job layoff) or you run into some essential but unexpected expenses (car breaks down, health expenses, etc.). It also allows you to save for things you know you will experience at some time in the future. If you know in a year you will need new tires for your car, start setting aside money now, and when the time comes, you will not need to buy them on credit. Once you have your savings bucket filled, you should have less financial stress because you know it is there to protect you.

I also recommend having a few extra special compartments in your savings bucket for specific life enhancement purposes.

The first special compartment in your savings bucket is a *just for me/fun indulgences* budget. Beyond your everyday expenses like food/housing/transportation/insurance, which come out of your spending bucket, I believe it is essential to also set aside money for things you enjoy or a way to chase your dreams. I choose to think about this in the savings bucket rather than spending bucket because it may be that you choose to save up over time for something special (a fancy new dress you really want or a vacation you desire your family to take). Setting a budget for these ensures that you don't overspend on these extras, yet are able to prioritize the little pleasures that are meaningful to your lifestyle. By saving for these indulgences before you purchase them, you are not

incurring any additional expense for interest on the purchase, but delaying gratification until you have the money and choose to spend what you have budgeted/saved wisely. With this savings approach, I believe you appreciate these indulgences more.

A second compartment in your savings bucket that I recommend is your *personal education* budget. In my opinion, people should always be investing in themselves. When a certain amount of money is budgeted for networking, books, courses, special training, mastermind groups etc., you will target improving your capabilities to be more productive and possibly earn more in the future. Knowledge/special skills (I call this intellectual capital) are something that can never be taken away from you. If you plan and budget these educational expenses, you can pursue an intentional plan of development and not fall into the trap of many people who spend thousands of dollars on educational events, yet never start to apply what they have learned. I clearly look for a return on investment in my educational expenses.

History shows that people who have created significant wealth often tend to be people who have also failed along the way, sometimes multiple times in their lives. Perhaps this is the case because they are trying new things out, blazing new trails, doing things in ways never tried before. Clearly no one wants to lose money, but these are often situations where the potential returns are very substantial, where you might be able to earn 10X or 20X your investment. You often "pay your dues" in learning what doesn't work or building your skills to discover what does work. If you choose to invest in education from an expert in a certain area, you are less likely to have big failures and more likely to rebound quicker from setbacks. This rebound-ability comes from education/experience and represents the critical importance of building one's intellectual capital, as well as one's financial capital.

I have also found that these educational experiences also tend to be the place I'm meeting ambitious people who think the same way I do. On many occasions I've developed friendships, as well as opportunities to do business together. So I also believe this educational budget is a prime way to develop one's relationship capital as well.

A third compartment of your savings bucket may be putting money aside for your children's *college education*. This can be a very significant expense, and one needs to prioritize how much one is willing to fund this, while at the same time, also making progress in funding one's own retirement account. Both may be essential, but don't make the mistake of thinking you can address all of your retirement needs after your children are through school.

The third overall bucket is your *INVESTMENT* account, the primary focus of this book. It represents how you choose to set up money working for you and is intended to compound into future wealth and prosperity. *The overall principal of this book is the harder/more efficiently you can get your money working for you in your investment bucket, the quicker you will reach the point of financial freedom and being able to focus your time on those activities in your life that allow you to make your greatest contributions to others.*

Decisions related to your investment plan should be made from the long-term perspective (at least 10-20 years out). During the pre-retirement accumulation phase, you should have a plan to continually funnel new savings into this bucket each month or year, as well as to allow the balance to compound. I believe you should treat invested funds as a protected sanctuary, never to be diminished with distributions for current consumption before retirement. If you face financial challenges along the way, you may need to stop adding to your retirement savings account for a period of time, but it is a major setback if you take distributions early.

While in this analogy, it helps to visualize this as a third investment bucket, which only accepts excess flows from above. From a practical standpoint, when you are planning and budgeting, you must figure out what you need to be adding to your investment account every quarter/year to achieve your desired end point—not just accepting what happens to overflow. Knowing what the gap between what your plan calls for and what your current lifestyle choices provide may help you make better decisions. Choosing to spend a little less now, so you can build up your retirement account, is a very prudent planning approach. Finding ways to earn more to fill this gap is an even better approach.

Realizing it is tough to "cut" expenses from one's current budget, there is a very smart approach to save more in the future. If you receive a pay raise, take a 2nd job or have a cash influx event such as getting a tax refund or making a profit on the sale of an investment, identify a certain percentage of the gain that will automatically go into your investment bucket. You will not feel it as a loss because you didn't previously depend on it. It is incremental to your current budget. I believe that 33%-50% of these incremental cash flow events is an appropriate amount to target into your investment account.

The way to quickly fill this third investment bucket is to ensure it is as efficient as possible, without incurring unreasonable risk. Efficiency = working harder. What this means is if money can grow in a tax advantaged structure, it will grow faster. If you are contributing more new capital in each month automatically, it will grow faster. If your investment yields are higher, it will grow faster. If you have less expense in fees, it will grow faster. If you protect the downside, and there is less volatility with proper asset allocation, it will grow faster across all market cycles. My key insight is that *if you can stack multiple benefits together…it will*

grow MUCH FASTER. It will truly become Harder Working Money.

However, the big caveat is to *protect the downside because if you lose significant capital, it is even harder to earn it back*. This is simple math. Let's say you had built up $100,000 in the stock market in 2008 when it crashed, and you happened to lose 50% of your money. At that point, you only had $50,000 remaining in the account. To get it back to $100,000 you need to re-earn 100% growth on your remaining account, and of course, that can take several years, possibly a decade depending on the growth rate of the rebound. To get to the point you hoped to be by that future date, you would probably need to quadruple your capital growth— probably an unrealistic expectation unless you learn to create substantial new value in new ways.

The key consideration is that after a big loss you need to earn much higher rates to recapture your desired position. Sizable losses need to be avoided at all costs; that is simple to say, but more difficult to do. Smaller losses can be limited with effective risk mitigation measures in the way you structure the deals.

A key element of your retirement plan should be how to *protect downside risk*. I believe that this is the part of planning that most people fail to consider and most don't know how to address. If you are buying individual stocks, you can put in trailing stop losses. If you are buying mutual funds, there are sophisticated hedges and options you can learn to apply. If you are buying real estate for rentals, make sure that you structure the acquisition with sufficient protective equity, at least 150% debt coverage on the cash flow and that you are not over leveraging. If you are involved with private lending, make sure there is plenty of protective equity and you understand the true values of the property and skills of the borrower.

Warren Buffet is famous for saying there are only two rules of investing: "1. Don't lose money, 2. Don't forget rule number 1."

I have certainly lost money in investments; I am humbled by some of the foolish things I've done out of haste, poor research or just responding with emotions. I tried speculative endeavors that did not pan out. I have been taken advantage of by an evil person. But now I'm focused on learning/applying lessons of how to structure deals to protect the downside. I'm seeking greater control and more contingency plans. *I now believe the chief differentiator between a novice and a sophisticated investor is the ability to protect downside risk*. I am striving to be a sophisticated investor and help others achieve that status as well.

To complete the bucket analogy, it is important to comprehend that the investment bucket also generally has multiple compartments, each playing a strategic role. These often include *a safety/protection compartment* where the key benefit is to generate a conservative but consistent return in soft markets, as well as *a higher targeted growth compartment* where funds may compound at higher rates during the good times, but capital is more at risk of loss. The size of each of these compartments is related to your investment asset allocation strategy and willingness to accept some risk. The balance between growth and conservative options also tends to shift toward the conservative end the more you have accumulated and the older you are.

In summary, a prudent approach of the buckets approach is to *make the spending bucket large enough to enjoy life, yet small enough so overflow continually fills the savings and investing buckets, too*. Then continually strive to *increase the income flowing into the top as much as possible*, either through increases in active income or adding multiple streams of passive income. You can also increase the flow by reducing taxes. Utilize your savings bucket only as back up for emergencies or to accumulate

planned future expenses. And learn the strategies of safely and securely growing your investment bucket as efficiently as possible, turning that capital into Harder Working Money.

Where Does Your Money Flow?

After assessing several income statements and balance sheets, Robert Kiyosaki teaches that people's money flows in different directions. The poor often have all of their income going straight out immediately as cash spending, with no savings or investments. The middle class typically have part of their income going directly to savings, but they often add assets and liabilities related to an improving lifestyle. When they buy a nice house and cars, these tend to be purchased on credit, which adds liabilities and increases expenses, so there is only a modest amount left for longer term saving and investing. Finally, the wealthy tend to do things differently. Rather than just spending their income directly, they often invest in income producing assets first. They then target some of the cash flow generated from these assets to pay for lifestyle expenses and other income to invest in additional investments. In this way, they may be gaining income and tax benefits, as well as building additional equity over time. Or as I like to say, *"stacking the benefits on the cash flow that naturally flows through their lives."*

I've discovered that a focused strategy of adding streams of passive income can create a rushing waterfall effect filling all the buckets. That is the primary strategy of wealth building that I have chosen, directing my capital into cash flow becoming Harder Working Money. However, I realize this more active investor approach may not be preferred by many people. This book attempts to explain the possibilities of becoming passive investors in privately structured deals through partnering or joint ventures,

and it also covers insights on efficiency of traditional Wall Street investment approaches as well, for your possible benefit.

Creating Wealth Requires Consistently Following a Plan

Unless you inherit wealth or are fortunate with a business startup, creating prosperity is typically the destination of a long journey. However, a sad fact is most people don't even create a plan—and even fewer are following in footsteps of people who have been successful in generating wealth and demonstrate a specific path they have selected. I suggest that both of these are prudent approaches.

The quickest and least risky approach to manifesting the life you desire is to find people who have already achieve what you are striving for and model their behavior.

If you have clarity of your path and confidence, it can succeed because you are following the guidance of others who have done what you strive to do, and I believe you are more likely to stay the course and achieve your desired outcome. Success is achieved in the follow-through on your plan, not just in the dreams of what could be.

In planning, it's critical for you to learn which types of investments make sense for your particular situation/strategy and which do not. Some of it just relates to personal interests—some assets are compelling for emotional reasons. I met a person who is heavily invested in alternative energy because this is his passion, while many other friends focus on private lending because they perceive significant upside to this involvement in real estate without all the downside drama of owing rental properties.

From my vantage point, investment opportunities are just like taking the subway. Go to the station and you have lots of options. To take the right train you need first to clarify where you want to go and when you need to get there. There are an abundance of opportunities to consider, but many are just distractions because they can't get you to where you want to go efficiently. Just because you see many people chasing after one train or another, doesn't necessarily make it right for you. If you miss one train, another will show up in a few minutes—never chase one because you are rushing thinking you are missing out, or you may discover this one takes you to an undesired destination.

Take your time; feel comfortable that you know that there is clear plan alignment and that the facts of the case support reasonable risk and reward. Figure out how specific assets may benefit in achieving your goals for specific purposes. If you discover that non-traditional investment opportunities may be better aligned to achieve your goals, get the proper guidance on how to pursue these investments from people experienced in the area. If you prefer to stick with Wall Street type of investments, just be sure that you are minimizing fees and not paying someone year after year to deliver sub-optimal results.

Sophisticated investors and their advisors clearly understand the attributes and benefits of one investment class over another, as well as what reasonable returns are typical in that class. They know the potential shortfalls that can impede results. Then they are able to determine whether a supposed opportunity is right for their specific situation, and if the currently available price is attractive or not. Only when all the stars align should you move forward. Only then should you take bold purposeful action with the confidence you are on the right path.

"Let the game come to you. You set the rules of when you play and how you play... when you invest... how much you invest...

what time you actually go into the market. These are the things you can control."

One thing about investing is you have almost an unlimited number of investment options. While some consider this intimidating/fearful, I will share what I've discovered about a variety of investment options to help broaden your perspective. As well I'll expose you to options you may not even know exist. Let your education help narrow the field. There are an unlimited number of places you can gain additional perspectives as well. Even though you may not be infatuated with the topic, like I have become, you need to gain at least a peripheral understanding of financing your retirement and learn who you can trust for guidance.

As I said before, realize all points of view contain biases. I'm not trying to "sell" you that my perspective on pursuing income producing assets is right for you, just to explain why I have chosen it to be right for me. Ask 100 financial advisors or friends for their opinion on proper investment planning, and you will certainly get 100 different answers. My purpose is trying to help you become better informed so you can ask better questions and then decide what is right for your family. I'm hopeful that the insights provided herein will help you better understand that which is unclear for many.

As previously stated, I believe wealth must generally be created, not earned. In other words, without 40 years or more to reach your goal, if your plan is only to invest modest amounts in traditional securities, your plan is primarily buying income/protecting capital—not creating equity/building a huge capital base. With this plan, it will be very difficult to achieve true prosperity in a reasonable period of time. On the other hand, if you create or participate in privately structured deals where the rewards can be high relative to the risk accepted, and you structure the deal

including the use of other people's money, you are more likely to build a substantial income and portfolio value in a much shorter period of time.

Once you've determined an opportunity is consistent with your strategy and attractive...then commit to the right size of investment in that specific opportunity. It is prudent to never risk too much of one's seed corn in any one particular investment. Spreading your money across several assets is a preferred risk mitigating technique.

Once you have clarified your plan and have had initial success in one area, your next appropriate step is to replicate that success over and over. It is the time to pursue mastery in this specific area. Be fruitful and multiply! Don't get distracted by other shiny objects, just consistently do the things that you know are moving you toward your goal. People who chase too many new approaches often lose what they have gained in one area in another they do not yet fully understand.

I recommend you evaluate several possible avenues for investing and select one as your primary path. Just be sure that your chosen path has a reasonable expectation of getting you to your destination. Be sure that you understand how this investment can generate the profits you seek. Laser sharp focus creates power in what you do and leads to mastery.

Realize the road to prosperity is likely to be a long journey, but a trip worth taking. Certainly, you must break down your plan into a progression of milestone achievements. Once you first generate a retirement portfolio, which in addition to your expected Social Security payments will provide the income for your bare necessities (food/shelter/health care/transportation and the basic monthly expenses of life), you should be able to sleep stress free. And once you have success in this level of achievement, you will

likely be emboldened to continue to build your portfolio to additionally provide for the lifestyle desires that make life more joyful. And finally, if you become wildly successful in your investments, you will be able to leave a legacy benefitting generations to come.

In addition, if you have a business that covers many expenses that impact your lifestyle (a business cell phone, a business car, travel, education) or invest in assets which generate sheltered income streams, your long-term capital needs may be significantly less. Do this all with tax and fee efficiency, and you are truly stacking the benefits for significant advantage.

The Right Strategies for the Right Time of Life

In traditional financial planning, there are generally two life phases to consider, with appropriate but different strategies in each phase:

1. The accumulation/wealth building phase
2. The retirement lifestyle and health maintenance distribution phase

The reason these two phases are recommended to have different strategies is that most people will have greater risk tolerance when they are younger and in the accumulation phase than once they are in retirement. This is only natural. If you are 25-45 and have several decades until you plan to retire, even should your investment portfolio suffer a major crash in the markets, you still have significant time to rebound. As well, younger people's primary focus is building wealth, so a more aggressive posture is appropriate. However, if you are 65+ and already taking distributions from your account, you more likely want to be positioned more conservatively to not put what you have already accumulated at risk.

For those who are very successful, you may also graduate onto a third phase of legacy building and preservation where the focus is on building and preserving generational wealth that will survive well after you pass away.

Accumulation & Wealth Building Phase

For most people, in the late first trimester and middle trimester of life, establishing routine savings with a specific plan toward wealth creation should become a primary focus. It's the game of generating active income in excess of your desired lifestyle needs today and investing it in ways that, in the long run, you have distributions or passive income streams to meet your future desired lifestyle burn rate.

Sage advice is that the earlier you start and more consistent you are in making contributions, the more the power of compounding will work for you and multiply your savings. Of course, the decision to delay gratification when you are younger is a difficult thing to do. Many are paying off college loans, spending to form families and buy their 1st home, spending to fill that home with furniture and all the necessities of life. But as I have demonstrated, simply choosing to start to put away a small amount each week has significant benefits over the long run, and it's a great habit to instill early in life.

There are several different investment strategies that you can pursue during the accumulation phase. Most employees get involved in a 401K plan at work, which can be a wise approach, provided your company is matching contributions. Participation in these plans is like earning free extra investment capital in the company match, a benefit your company offers but only contributes to those who choose to participate in the program. The

primary benefit of a 401K or an IRA plan (and the other corresponding plans dependent on your type of employment) is that you can grow your retirement savings in a tax advantaged environment.

At the same time, I don't believe it is prudent to *only* max out your annual 401K contribution limit and feel you are on plan. If you haven't worked through a personal investment plan, you might be congratulated for taking the first step of putting something away, but you are really shooting in the dark in regard to reaching future prosperity. In my opinion, lack of planning is a reason so many fall short in properly funding their retirement. When they near retirement age and begin to study what they have accumulated vs. what they really need, too many are discovering "Oops, too little...too late. Now what do I do?"

If you are a business owner/professional or entrepreneur fully responsible for your own retirement planning, your options and priorities are likely to be much different than a traditional employee. You often must decide "should I invest more into the current needs of growing the business or contribute more into my retirement plan?" This is where education becomes even more critical. Think through the pros and cons of multiple options. Rather than just accept a foundation of what someone else has chosen for you—when you are able to comprehend a broader array of options—you can more diligently plan for and execute a specific retirement plan directed to your personal situation, while you also take care of your business. You need a retirement plan with a reasonable expectation to fully fund the lifestyle to which your family has become accustomed, regardless of the performance of your business.

Also, as a business owner/professional, it is wise to *figure out an exit from your business* in the long run—many find out they have golden handcuffs beyond the point they would prefer to walk away

because they never started a Plan B to sustain passive income without the business. Too many small businesses are difficult to sell without the key rainmaker, so don't presume that just because you have a viable business it has significant value when you want to leave it.

IRA's/401K's...Traditional and Roth

Everyone who chooses to utilize a traditional 401K or IRA invests with pretax dollars. This program enables you to get a tax deduction today, which can help you invest more and build your portfolio value quicker. Another important consideration of traditional IRA's/401K's is to not be deceived by the bigger numbers growing in your account balance. In these plans, the IRS is essentially your investment partner for life. When it comes time to distribute from the plan, the IRS will have their hand out to take their appropriate share down the road. This will likely be 25-35% of your total distribution. Don't be shocked if this is the cake that you baked; plan for it when you evaluate how much your account is growing and the total accumulation you need to fund your future lifestyle.

Alternatively, if you invest in a Roth 401K or IRA, you are funding with after tax dollars and all of the compounded growth of your money will be tax free. The difference is whether you choose to pay the tax on the seeds or on the harvest—whether the IRS is your partner benefiting from the growth of your account, or if you and your family will be the sole beneficiaries. Utilizing a Roth IRA/401k requires you to pay more in taxes today, so the amount left over for savings will be limited. However, everything you grow from that point forward is yours alone.

As you have seen in some of the examples in the prior chapter, being more efficient in taxes and compounding money over the long-term can make very significant differences in results. Some financial planners believe that *the Roth IRA option is the greatest tax loophole that the majority of Americans are qualified to take advantage of, yet few utilize this benefit*. Have you even considered how this type of conversion or funding approach could benefit you?

It generally is possible to convert funds from a traditional 401K/IRA account into a Roth account, provided you pay the taxes on the rollover. A Roth conversion is simply giving the IRS back their share today, so they will no longer be your partner in the future. Depending on how you feel about the likelihood taxes will go up in the future, this may be a prudent thing to consider, particularly if you gain a windfall of capital to pay the taxes. And rollovers don't need to be all taken at one time.

There are currently only two restrictions to consider if planning to convert funds into a Roth account. The first is that you must wait five years after converting the account before withdrawing any gains. And second, your annual income can't exceed $100,000 during any year you make a Roth conversion.

I'd suggest, whenever possible, working with your financial advisor to consider how you can use a little excess money today in paying taxes on a rollover to move part of your retirement account into a tax-free place to compound your investment capital. Just remember that the longer you wait to convert a traditional IRA over to a Roth, the higher your account value will climb, and the more taxes you will have to pay either to convert it or when you start distributing it as income. Over the years, tax efficiency can make a huge difference in the longevity your retirement distributions will cover.

One benefit in converting portions of your account in smaller increments year after year is that you can strategically move a specific amount so you don't get bumped into a higher tax bracket. The IRS does consider an amount rolled over as income in the year of the conversion, so you want to make a conversion as efficiently as possible, since this is a taxable event.

Another advantage of Roth IRA/401K plans is that, unlike traditional plans, you don't face the same mandatory distributions from your plan in your 70's and beyond. With a Roth, you have more control…since the money is all yours. You don't have the IRS as a partner setting the rules of your distribution. You simply decide what is needed and write the checks when and how you desire.

From my point of view, a key problem with 401K's and IRA's (whether traditional or Roth) is that in their most utilized form your primary options are to only invest in mutual funds—it's often the only choice given. Mutual funds do provide a broad diversification of stock performance coverage; however, they basically lock you into the Wall Street Casino for life, along with all of its fees and limitations. So while I'm an advocate of participating in a plan if you are an employee for the company match—I would recommend doing so in a Roth plan if possible, and only contributing to the limit of their match, then putting all of your other savings, over that required for company match, into some other investment options.

If you have moved from company to company and can roll 401K balances into an IRA, an attractive consideration is to roll your money into a ***Self-Directed IRA*** or qualified retirement plan and get involved in a whole host of alternative investment options. ***I believe this is one of the most underutilized tools for effective retirement planning***. It's my understanding that less than 5% of IRA/401K holders have a self-directed account. Most people

outside of the real estate investing world I talk to have no idea what I'm talking about. If you are wondering what this is all about, I'd suggest it may represent a great opportunity for you to look into. Obviously, I prefer this approach rather than keeping retirement capital in company stock or a basket of mutual funds. I've been involved in both self-directed IRA's, as well as a new Qualified Retirement Plan in my business; both are greatly benefitting my Harder Working Money plan.

Recall that the basic principle of this book is that if you find ways to keep your money working harder, you will more quickly and certainly reach your financial freedom point. Properly utilizing tools such as tax advantaged savings environments and a broader array of investment options may enable a quicker path to prosperity, perhaps much earlier than the traditional retirement age.

Volatility of Markets—Should You Seek Diversification?

It is paramount to understand that *all financial market sectors go through cycles*. At times, one sector will be going up rapidly, while at other times, they are crashing back down. There certainly have been times when everything is dumping, but more often there are counter cyclical trends among sectors and different countries of the world. Big volatility (large gains and losses) and market cycles happen in stocks/mutual funds/precious metals/commodities. It happens much less frequently in bonds and some types of real estate, which provide a more reliable or stated return. Annuities are a unique asset class because they have no volatility; they are a contract with stated returns.

The timing of when you buy, relative to the ups and downs of the market, can make a huge impact in your net returns; however; *NO*

ONE can predict when the market directional trends will shift. The smartest minds in investment proclaim "it's not an issue of whether the markets will crash again, just when." And turn on a talking heads finance show and you will get two people looking at the exact same facts, predicting contrary expectations for what will happen next. Don't try to outsmart the big money on market timing—time and time again proves they really don't know either.

The key insight that I take from this is that if you choose to play in the Wall Street casino, *you shouldn't try to time the market cycles and shift investment strategies from time to time.* If you try this you are just as likely to be wrong as correctly predict the shift and experience missed opportunities or big losses. In my opinion it is far better to *devise a financial strategy that can work moderately well across all market cycles*. This structure is attempting to balance your portfolio risk so in all environments something is doing well—and to the best of your ability you are protecting the downside such that, when some asset classes are out of favor, you limit your losses while other classes are providing offsetting gains.

Theoretically, this may be like choosing the turtle over the hare in a race. Yes, when everything seems to be going up in the stock market, you are giving up yield to have much of your money in other asset classes that are generating modest returns. However, remember what we demonstrated about the severe long-term penalty of losing your investment capital. One thing we all know about the stock market is that it cycles through ups and downs: Bull market (+) and Bear market (-) cycles, often every 4-8 years.

It is also important to realize that, beyond cyclical shifts in market demand driven by the overall economy/demographics that impact business results, there are also market swings impacted by outside policy influences. When the Federal Reserve decided to pull back inter-bank interest rates to less than 1% for the past five years, a lot of money shifted out of bonds and into the stock market, chasing

yield. This increased demand for stocks substantially, and many feel it is responsible for the big bull market that has happened since mid-2009, driving up the Dow 130%. In order to protect your downside, it is wise to maintain a fifty thousand foot perspective in trying to understand why conditions are occurring as they are as well as how likely they are to be maintained in the future. Taking the long-term perspective on what is driving or hindering markets and following a stable plan can help you moderate emotional trading.

It's human nature to buy and sell on emotion. The experience of most people is that, when something has been going up and up for a period, you want to jump in on the band wagon and buy more only to discover that it has started to fall. Then when you see values going down and down, you fear you'll lose it all and sell near the bottom.

This tendency is so prevalent that a recent study by a research firm Dalbar shows that, while the S&P 500 has increased in value 9.2% annually over the past two decades, the average stock market investor realized only a 2.5% net return during this same period (giving up nearly 3/4 of the underlying market gain before taxes)! Reportedly, there as three primary reasons for this shortfall: 1. Emotional buying on the highs and selling on the lows with a chasing yield strategy. In fact, one research study demonstrated that 96% of managed funds underperform the broad market indexes over a 10 year span. The president of Dalbar says, "Most investors, including fund managers, move their money in and out at the wrong times…they get excited or panic and these trades really hurt their overall performance." 2. Fees that go to portfolio managers, financial institutions and transactional costs can eat up a huge portion of the gains. 3. There is a minor statistical effect, which exaggerates the difference between the S&P and individual investors, since not all people were in the market for the whole

period and the S&P has experienced a couple of long bull markets during these two decades. At any rate, the Dalbar study certainly proves that *simply buying and holding the broad index of the whole market produces much better/more consistent results than actively managed funds of individual stocks*—and of course, from a fee perspective, this is a much less expensive option.

One of the key reasons people recommend diversifying your investment portfolio across several market sectors/asset classes is that different sectors tend to have different rates of volatility and get pushed up or down in different economic conditions. For example, during some times when stocks and commodities are hot, bonds have very little growth. However, in a different situation, when the stock market crashes and commodity prices go down, bonds become a place of safety. And when stocks, commodities and bonds are all crashing,...precious metals like gold tend to spike dramatically in value. There are many active ways to hedge risk, but broad diversification is a key recommended strategy for traditional investors.

When you have a diversified, balanced portfolio you end up minimizing your risk of loss through normal market cycles. However, don't be misled by the term balanced portfolio. I believe if you are pursuing this approach you should strive to balance the overall risk profiles of each of the portfolio assets, not the value attributed to each sector. In other words, since history demonstrates that stocks tend to be 3X more volatile than bonds, having much more money in bonds than stocks would be a way to balance the volatility risk of your overall portfolio.

For those of you interested in sticking to Wall Street assets rather than privately structured off-market deals, one of the best performing portfolio allocation models is reported to be Ray Dalio's All Weather Fund, discussed in Tony Robbins's great book *Money: Master the Game*. The All Weather Fund was specifically

designed to reduce the effects of market volatility and perform well across all market conditions. It was designed to be set up once and never have the allocation changed. This asset allocation calls for 30% stocks (in a broadly diversified index), 15% in intermediate bonds (7-10 year Treasuries), 40% in long-term bonds (20-25 year Treasuries), 7.5% in gold and 7.5% in commodities. When back testing this portfolio's performance over the past 30 years, it generated 9.7% annual return making money 86% of the time. It demonstrated very little risk and low volatility. Quite a stellar performance.

I believe if I were in a position of already having a couple of million or more in investible assets, I would strongly consider allocating a large part of my retirement account in this way as a passive investor, because the All Weather Allocation has been proven to generate strong returns with very modest risk across all market cycles. However, since I'm still in the accumulation phase, I have selected an alternate active investor path pursuing private deals outside of the markets as my preferred plan. Perhaps, in time, my situation or yours will change. If so, remember this attractive safe harbor for passive investors with significant capital.

Traditional Asset Options During Accumulation

Once you have decided to jump into the savings game (or dramatically alter your current approach), then you need to decide your new investing philosophy. What assets will you choose to invest in and why? And what allocation decisions will you apply across investment sectors?

Wall Street isn't the only game in town, as will be discussed later in this book; however, I do recognize this is where most of the money is today, and we should inform of options/strategies here

for the typical retirement saver that may have little or no initial interest in learning about privately structured deals.

Stocks, mutual funds, bonds and treasury notes all come in tens of thousands of options for the passive investor. In a broad sector like stocks, you can invest in different market sectors like big blue chip companies (the largest companies and brands) that tend to pay consistent dividends (payments every quarter basis their excess profits) or in the leading companies that dominate market sectors (healthcare/banking/consumer products/housing/industrial sectors). Some people prefer the smaller companies, which don't tend to offer dividends but whose upside potential for growth may be greater. You can choose to invest in individual companies or mutual funds that own a broad selection of companies' stock that you can acquire the whole basket just by owning one share of the index fund. The options are endless.

Of course the typical answer for most people is to take the easy way out. Check a box on a form and distribute your money in an array of mutual funds and then → hope for the best over time.

As I previously reported from the Dalbar study, *one desirable and efficient way to participate in the stock market is to purchase a broad index*, for example the most popular one is based on the Standard & Poor's 500 Index. This is a composite of the capitalization of 500 of the largest companies on the US stock exchanges. One clear benefit of participating in this index is that it is broadly diversified across many market sectors with large cap companies. While you don't get full upside potential of superstar companies, you also don't take the risk of having all of your money tied up in just a few companies that can experience tough times/significant market price declines. An index will be far less volatile than a portfolio of a handful of stocks in individual companies and is an effective risk mitigation technique—as well as a way to greatly reduce fees. Its performance is basis the

understanding that American businesses tend to grow over time as they create value/leverage resources.

For even broader participation across all sized companies, there is the Willshire 5000, which owns a majority of the stocks available, including many smaller companies. If you prefer smaller companies' stocks the Russell 2000 includes 2000 of the best performing smaller companies. The granddaddy of all indexes is the Dow Jones Industrial Average. It is comprised of 30 of the largest and most influential companies; however, I believe it has truly become meaningless over the past several decades. As companies merge and go out of business or new ones experience stratospheric growth, the makeup of the Dow changes. While it continues to represent about 25% valuation of all equities, from a historical perspective, the included companies are always different. Many of the superstars 50 years ago no longer exist. Therefore, I believe tracking it is of marginal benefit, yet this is what leads the financial news every night.

I have never purchased a bond and am not really in a position to add insights on them; however, should you choose to structure a Wall Street based portfolio, you will need bonds in the mix to mitigate market-based risk. There are a variety of sectors in bonds. You can buy bonds from all over the world. Emerging market bonds are often touted as a good place to get a higher yield. Some bonds are for a short timeframe, while others are designed for a longer-term hold. Some municipal bonds receive special tax advantages that increase your net effective yield. Should you choose to invest in bonds, the same basic sound investing principles would apply. Purchase a mixture of multiple assets, and find ways to minimalize fees.

On gold and commodities, I really have little to add as well. I used to own a fair quantity of silver and gold; however, when it kept losing value and not earning any cash flow, I decided to sell and

put my money into something I trust will make me money today. Anxious for growth, I lost interest in using precious metals as an insurance policy to protect value. If the world economies start crashing, maybe I will wish I had held on to metals for the spike. I will say, if you desire to hold gold, I'm a strong proponent of physical gold bullion over numismatic coins (collectables) and certainly over tracking stocks like GLD. If the shit hits the fan and gold spikes 10X over a short period of time, you will want physical possession and have something that is easily traded to take some of these gains off of the table before the price deflates again. Bullion is liquid (easily sold) and fungible (easily valued/substituted).

The Devastating Results of Mutual Funds

You, no doubt, have sensed that I am no longer a fan of mutual funds. For years, I was naive and didn't understand the real proposition. At one point, I had a lot of my retirement capital in mutual funds, just like most people currently do. Because this is a path so many others are traveling, I'd like to explain the downside I now perceive in professionally managed mutual funds. It seems clear to me now that these are set up to benefit the big Wall Street financial institutions, and hoodwink most of their clients. I believe it's time clients understand the undeniable facts.

I judge there are 3 reasons most people choose to participate in managed mutual funds:

1) They often are the primary options to choose among on your company's 401K election form or in the IRA's from big Wall Street financial institutions.
2) They are an asset class that provides diversification in identifiable sectors of the stock market and are being actively managed by so-called experts—i.e. at first glance

they sound attractive and seem to be a responsible way to invest.

3) Everyone else seems to be invested there, and Wall Street certainly promotes them. They are an easy choice for the passive investor (who doesn't know any better) to just make the popular and easy choice.

What I believe you should comprehend is that data suggests managed mutual funds are a loser bet for 4 primary reasons:

1) Compounding fees suck up most of the gains over the long-term (math that will likely confound you as explained below).What you think you are earning is always much more than what you end up with in your account balance.

2) Because individual stocks in a managed fund are constantly churning, even if you hold the fund for the long-term, you will be hit with annual earned income taxes on the gains, rather than capital gains in the long run. This deflates your earnings and delays the power of compounding.

3) The vast majority of managed funds historically underperform the broad market on a net basis over the long-term, the exact opposite of what you would expect when "professionals" are managing your money. It has been documented that 96% of managed funds fail to achieve the broad market performance over a 10 year period on a net basis in one study, while other studies reported this shortfall was over 80%. Yes, every year there are positive stand outs; however, the funds that stand out one year don't seem to be consistently performing well over time (other than a small handful of superstar/closed funds only available to the ultra-wealthy who have hundreds of millions of dollars to invest). Picking mutual funds on the basis of Morningstar's 5 star ratings has been

compared to driving by looking only into your rear view mirror.

4) You can't mitigate the downside using trailing stop losses on mutual funds like you can on individual stocks.

When I first heard the compounding effect of fees on long-term valuation by Jack Bogle, CEO of Vanguard Funds, I simply didn't believe what he was claiming. The math felt just wrong. So I sat down with a calculator and, after a half hour of playing, I had convinced myself he is absolutely right. If you would like to hear a PBS interview with Jack discussing the peril of fees on mutual funds, just search on Google for "Frontline + Jack Bogle." This program was titled "The Retirement Gamble" and aired April 23, 2013.

It is clearly something people who currently own mutual funds need to comprehend. At any rate, here goes a story of confounding math…and the way Wall Street stacks the deck and skims off most of the investors' profits.

Research across a variety of classes of managed mutual funds shows that the total average annual cost of participation is 3.17%. (Fees are often about two-thirds of this, but what matters are the total costs charged to your account.) You may think that your funds are charging less; however, many of the fees and trading charges are hidden or named in ways to keep you from thinking they are fees on your statements or in the fund brochures. Even if yours is less, this number will not be far off. It has been reported that a PhD in economics took months of researching to discover all the true fees on his mutual fund account. He located over 17 fees being charged to his account. He found, "asset management fees, 12/b-1 marketing fees, trading costs, market impact costs, soft-dollar costs, redemption fees, account fees, purchase fees, record keeping fees, plan administration fees and on and on."

The 3.17% average fee is about 25 times as much as you would pay in fees to participate in a non-managed index fund of the broad market. And this is just for the fund. If you hold your mutual funds in a 401K or IRA account, there is an additional 1.13% fee, on average, for administrative costs of the account, regardless of the fees of the assets the account holds.

At first glance these fees sound small: 3.17% or 1.13%. What you may fail to realize is these costs impact your account balance every year whether your account value is up, down or sideways. They are not just added to new funds being contributed to, but on your entire account balance. Again and again and again your account is charged, and the effects of the fees compound over the years. The resulting effect is that the fees really stifle your account growth. Depending on the specific performance of your funds over time, fees will end up absorbing about two-thirds or more of the potential gains in the funds. Let me be clear. You put up 100% of the money and take 100% of the risk. But at the end of the day, over the long run, it's set up so the "house" takes between 60-70% of the gain, and you net only about 30-40%. (The Las Vegas casinos would be so envious if they were able to set these odds!)

What if there are no profits some years because the market crashes? Your account goes down even more than the market decline because the ongoing, compounding fees are taken out regardless.

Here is an example to clarify the impact of fees over time. Let's say you have $100,000 lump sum (one time) to invest and leave it compounding for 30 years to fund your retirement. This example assumes an average annual return of 8% on a gross basis. If you didn't have any fees or taxes, as a baseline, $100K/30 years at 8% compounded would be a gross total possible of $1,006,266. Seems pretty impressive at first doesn't it? Ten times growth in 30 years with no additional contributions.

Now we will compare 3 options, each the net result of the 8% gross return less fees/taxes:

- If you invested in a very low fee index fund in an IRA (tax free or tax deferred), and your net return was 6.7% (1.3% fee total), your value after 30 years would grow to $699,733 or a net cost of just over 30%. (Note: most of this is for the administrative fee for the IRA, the cost of the fund is about .2%.)
- If your IRA (1.1% fee) invested in a mutual fund (3.1% fee) for a net return of 3.8%, your value after 30 years would grow to only $306,140 or a net cost of over 69%.
- If you invest non-tax deferred money into the same fund, and only net 3.1% return because of the tax effect in annual compounding, your value after 30 years would only grow to $249,896 or a net cost of about 75%!

So the net story on mutual funds is you can pay much more for a professional to manage your money, have up to a 96% chance of underperforming the market in general and also pay more in taxes. Look again at the difference between the index fund and the managed account results: $699,733 vs. $306,140— over double the results assuming the same baseline 8% account growth before fees. Do mutual funds still sound like a good investment choice?

A basic heuristic to remember is for every 1% in fees on a going basis, Wall Street will skim off at least 20% of your long-term gain—2% in fees a minimum of 40%, 3% in fees 60% +.The math just boggles my mind. It is a scam that nearly 100 million people are falling for, and investing trillions of dollars in assets in. All the while, the fancy investment bankers get their multi-million dollar annual bonuses, live in their mansions and vacation homes, drive their Mercedes or Porches and live the high life on the people who fell for the sucker's bet. Not me...no more!

Distribution and Health Maintenance Phase

In an ideal world, the final trimester of life would be stress-free and spent enjoying the bountiful harvest of what we have accomplished in the first 2/3 of our lives. However, for too many people, this will not be the case because of insufficient funding or inefficient compounding of their retirement account. A common fear of Baby Boomers today is that they will outlive their money. The ideal of enjoying time and financial freedom is what is causing me to sprint to the finish to attempt to prepare this outcome for my family during my remaining active investor role. I'm striving to enable my money to work harder, so I won't have to throughout my retirement years. Hopefully some of the insights and concepts of this book will have you better prepared when that time comes for you, as well.

The foundational principle of traditional retirement planning is you work, save and invest, accumulating a large portfolio during your working years that can be slowly disbursed to sustain your lifestyle through your retirement years. Climb the mountain on the way up through savings in your active income years, and then descend the mountain with retirement distributions.

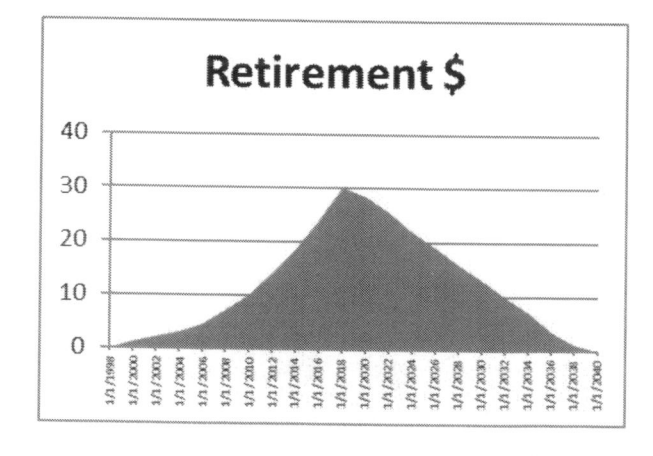

Traditional Approach to Accumulation and Distribution

As we've discussed, challenges to this plan are that many are living longer (yea), which means we need to fund a much longer lifetime of expenses (oops). Since most people have now been transitioned out of company-sponsored pension plans where the company had the obligation to figure out how to fund for their remaining lives, it is now up to each of us to take personal control and be sure we are adequately preparing to manage what we have accumulated and make it last however long our disbursement period may be. We also have to try to work the plan, so we are able to maintain the lifestyle that we have become accustomed to. No one wants to become a burden to our loved ones in our later years should we run out of money.

Of course, you are able to plan on supplementing your efforts with Social Security and Medicare program payments—but a key word is supplement. In no way should you presume that these programs will be sufficient to cover your lifestyle or health maintenance expenses alone.

An offsetting consideration is that if your retirement savings is in a traditional IRA/401K that has accumulated tax-free, you will still owe taxes on your distributions from your plan. In other words, let's say your financial plan suggests that you can maintain your desired lifestyle on $50,000/year beyond your annual Social Security distributions. This implies that you will need to pull about $75,000 per year from your nest egg in order to pay the government for their share of the plan distribution, depending on your tax bracket, and still have your $50,000 available for expenses.

A traditional heuristic that I've heard is that one should plan to distribute up to 4% of one's nest egg every year. In this way, provided your remaining portfolio is adequately protected from market crashes and continues to grow by at least the rate of inflation, each year your distribution would go up (year 2 $77,250,

year 3 $79,568, year 4 $81,954 assuming a 3% annual rate of inflation). Under this example's scenario, provided your account had reached a peak balance of $1,875,000, you could take out these annual distributions, pay your taxes and sustain these inflation protected disbursements for 25 years (65 years old → 90 years old). Of course this ideal scenario includes a lot of what ifs.

An alternate heuristic that I'm promoting in Harder Working Money is that you build a portfolio of cash flowing assets which generate your after tax desired lifestyle burn rate in monthly passive income. This is an entirely different approach to focus on income streams greater than what you spend on a monthly basis, not climb some huge mountain of equity. So if you need $4,166/month cash flow ($50,000/year) after tax, you would need up to $6,312/month pre-tax cash flow if the assets are held outside of an IRA/401K, or about $9,564/month if the assets are held in a tax advantaged environment from which you still need to pay Uncle Sam. From my perspective, this seems like a much more achievable plan in a reasonable period of time.

The key difference is that in the traditional alternative you are spending down your nest egg. In the Plan B scenario, you set up cash flow streams that are evergreen. You are receiving the monthly cash flow income of the assets to live on, but not needing to sell the assets to raid your capital accumulation. This requires a paradigm shift about retirement planning—it is a forward thinking approach.

One way that cash flow real estate really works in your favor is, if properly structured over time, your tenants are paying off the mortgage on your properties. So you may be receiving $220/month net income on a rental when you are covering the mortgage; however, later in your holding of the property, when the mortgage is eliminated, your net income may grow to $520/month once you own the property free and clear (without considering possible

inflationary growth of rents). So as your cost of living goes up over time, so can the productivity of your cash flowing assets.

Of course, a prudent plan is to probably have a mixture of both a portfolio of equity to be distributed, as well as income producing assets. As well, for the sake of safety, I'm striving to establish funding for a desired lifestyle burn rate about 50% higher than I really expect my family will need. I figure it's better to target more than we need than to find out inflation was higher or taxes become higher, etc.

I will admit, if you are nearing or in your distribution and health maintenance phase and need more clarity for a distribution plan primarily in Wall Street securities, you should be seeking guidance from other sources more experienced in this phase than I. Most of my study has been on how to accumulate the retirement nest egg/long-term cash flow, and that is where I believe I can currently provide greater value for others.

With the Plan B passive income approach I advocate, *the only real difference between accumulation and distribution is reaching that point where your passive income exceeds your desired lifestyle burn rate, and you no longer need to continue to add assets to your portfolio*. Cash flow income can be evergreen provided you care for the goose that lays the golden eggs.

Chapter 4—ADVANTAGES OF AN INCOME-ORIENTED INVESTMENT STRATEGY

It is never easy to decide to go against the traditional approach that everyone else seems to be using; however, I believe if you are open minded you will perceive that this alternative offers many advantages and a chance to play a winning hand in far less time.

Shifted Paradigms: Equity Appreciation vs. Cash Flow Income

My philosophy about a viable path to generating long-term prosperity has shifted and now is divergent from the mainstream. Most people follow the herd and plan that, during employment, savings will be set aside and invested to create a giant storehouse of equity from which to draw down distributions over retirement.

Plan A: Work/earn → Invest tax deferred 401K → Compound in mutual funds over the long -term seeking to build equity → Retire at 65 → Distribute retirement income/pay taxes → Hope the money lasts

In this approach, most people work as an employee or a self-employed professional and choose to invest for their retirement via a 401K in mutual funds. This may still be the best approach for you, provided you've been on this path for decades and your accumulation has achieved critical mass which means you are in the high growth part of the compounding curve. If that is so,

congratulations, perhaps some of the insights in this book will help you be more efficient, such as switching from mutual funds to a broad based low fee index fund or an insurance annuity, as well as converting at least a part of your IRA into a Roth IRA. If so, optimizing your plan may help it grow faster and cumulate more on a net basis, so you are more likely to have desirable options in retirement and not stress about outliving your money.

However, if you aren't well down the road on this approach, I recommend it is appropriate to consider shifting your focus from climbing the huge mountain of equity accumulation to building a portfolio of assets that reliably generate sustainable monthly cash flow streams. This income-oriented investment strategy is the path I feel is most appropriate for my family's current situation.

Plan B: Work/earn/at same time learn about cash flow investing → Continue to earn active income while also investing in cash flow assets (either as an active or passive partner in deals) → When passive cash flow > lifestyle expenses consider retiring from day job, regardless of age → Continue to build your portfolio with additional cash flow assets because it's fun to do → Save on tax sheltered income streams & and enjoy life → Leave your evergreen portfolio of cash flow assets to heirs or charity

Generating cash flow in your portfolio requires only two things:

1. Income generating assets (such as rental properties, private lending on investment properties or businesses)
2. Capital to buy the asset or the ability to borrow money at a rate at which the asset can pay for the loan/all asset expenses and still generate positive cash flow spreads

George Antone, the greatest financial mind I know, calls this duality concept **Wealth Pairs.** He recommends people become

wealth pair farmers in his exceptional book, *The Wealthy Code* and his follow-up book on private lending, *The Banker's Code*. I consider George my mentor, and he has been instrumental in helping me see the light in using the power of finance to win the prosperity game. He has helped me pursue advanced application of some of the basic principles I learned from Robert Kiyosaki's *Rich Dad Poor Dad*. Hopefully, the way I'm explaining some of his insights will help you comprehend this new alternative way to plan for your retirement funding as well.

When pursuing Plan B, whether your long-term after-tax desired lifestyle burn rate requirement (beyond Social Security) is targeted to be $5,000, $10,000, $20,000/month or more, once you have amassed a portfolio of wealth pairs generating this amount in recurring passive income, you achieve financial and time freedom. At that point, your choices are unconstrained.

It doesn't matter how much money you have had to borrow to generate this cash flow...as long as the assets continue to generate income beyond the expense of the mortgage, this debt is just an enabler. Robert Kiyosaki calls income producing mortgages "good debt" because it puts additional cash in your pocket. Appropriately using leverage helps you attain your goals much faster.

With Plan B, you will no longer need to be trading time for money in normal employment unless you choose to because you will no longer need the income from your job. Your cash flow investments will provide monthly mailbox money. Just like in Robert Kiyosaki's Cash Flow 101 board game, the objective is to get out of the rat race by investing in cash flow assets to set you free. And just like in the game when you reach the investor fast track, the lucrative opportunities available to experienced investors can be life altering and provide the opportunity to give more to others in your community.

If, like me, you are a late bloomer in shifting your retirement plan into high gear, it seems much more realistic to focus this year's investment target on "how can I safely and reliably add an additional $500-$2,000/month after tax positive cash flow to my financial engine?" rather than "how can I add an additional $50-100,000/year capital appreciation to my retirement nest egg trying to play catch up?" Provided you also buy into this logic, the strategies and vehicles discussed in this *Harder Working Money* book may become much more enlightening to you. And *the time horizon for you to achieve financial freedom may be in the next 5-10 years instead of the next 20-40 years*.

I prefer this income-oriented approach because I believe *it is a process in which I have much greater control*. One only needs to identify the best cash flow assets and the sources of funding required to acquire them. Through the power of finance and private investment opportunities anyone can learn to safely structure these wealth pairs to his or her advantage, maximizing returns and minimizing risk.

While single family rental properties have historically been the best-known cash flow producing investment asset, they certainly are not the only option. Others include commercial real estate, lending through private mortgages, businesses, insurance annuities, royalties or other limited partnership interests/private placements. Some people call these options Capital Assets because of their income orientation.

Key Distinctions/Benefits of Capital Assets

Capital assets are different than Wall Street financial securities in many ways. Wall Street securities tend to be very liquid (can be easily sold/converted to cash in minutes) and are fungible (one share of stock or bond is exactly the same as the next so its value is certain). On the other hand, *capital assets are unique and must be valued individually* (one business or rental property may be very different and have a different valuation than the next). Because of this, *they tend to be far less liquid than traditional financial securities* (may take months to sell if you need to liquidate).

There are several benefits to the active investor dealing in capital assets. Since they are unique, it takes local or specialized knowledge to differentiate the value of one asset versus a similar one. Perhaps this is an appraisal by a 3rd party. Perhaps it's just your ability to uncover opportunities looking at income statements and balance sheets. As an educated investor, you are able to generate substantial value just by locating great deals and sorting out the special opportunities from the people looking to sell at full value.

Since they are traded one by one, rather than like stocks in millions of shares a day, capital assets are always INEFFICIENT MARKETS. This can be a good thing for the individual investor; it means they are not something that the big money players can come in and dominate and manipulate (stack the deck against you). Capital assets are a great opportunity for the smaller player to *create real value in privately structured deals*. They are a great opportunity to shift the risk/reward paradigm for big returns but limited downside risk. *They are a great opportunity to fund your retirement in one-third the time.*

Since these assets must be bought and sold with unique transactions, it allows the specialist to find motivated sellers and

buy at a discount, obtaining instant gains in equity with the buy. (You can't buy stocks at a 10-30% discount on the going price of the day, but investment real estate trades that way every day). Inefficient markets allow you to privately structure deals for personal advantage and generate huge gains in equity just on how you buy. Building equity this way *can cut decades off of the timeline waiting for traditional securities to compound*.

Another differentiator of capital assets is *control*. With traditional Wall Street assets, your only decision is when to buy and when to sell. With capital assets, you are buying control. With control, you have *the ability to influence not only the return the asset generates, but also the value of the asset.* For example, if you purchase a distressed property at 30-50% of its optimal value because the house needs a lot of work, perhaps you get it fixed up for a total investment of only 65% of its value, and then you rent it out for cash flow. This enables you to *"create" substantial equity* in a very short period of time. This is called forced appreciation. An investor will never be able to force appreciation on a Wall Street security like you can on capital assets.

Along with this comes the responsibility of *managing the asset*. If your property management company does a great job of finding quality tenants and maximizing your rental income, the property will produce an above average ongoing return on the investment property. If not, you don't need to sell the property like you would with an underperforming stock, you just need to hire a better management company and transition the asset from a sub-optimal performer to a solid performer. *The ability to problem solve and retain assets is a substantial benefit to buy and hold investing*.

One of the biggest benefits to investing in capital assets is that they often can be *acquired using leverage*. This means if you want to buy a $70,000 rental property for the cash flow, you don't need to bring $70,000 cash to the closing table. Most rental properties are

purchased with a mortgage. So perhaps you are putting $14,000 (20%) down on the property and borrow the remainder from a bank. This allows you to control a much greater asset base with your available capital, and a larger asset base enables more monthly cash flow and possibly a greater return on your investment. As well, in the long run, possible appreciation really can magnify your benefits relative to the cash you have invested in the deals.

Buying fungible assets like Wall Street securities or precious metals with leverage is very tough to accomplish and this limits possible returns. As well given the volatility of these assets, buying on margin would also be extremely risky.

Properly used leverage generates a multiplying effect of the return on your capital and reduces the time it takes to reach your retirement plan/financial freedom goals. Just don't overdo it. Too high of leverage leaves you susceptible to loss during times the market may be dropping in value. Many people who became financially devastated during the housing bubble crash in 2008 were involved in very speculative transactions using very high leverage. The conservative approach to deal structuring is a more prudent approach.

Since *capital asset values are based on their inherent utility value* (ability to generate cash flow) *they tend to be good investment portfolio hedges against inflation*. When you own a rental property, over the long run, rents will rise with the rate of inflation. Perhaps the rent starts out at $800/month, but in less than a decade, it may be over $1,000/month. Correspondingly, since the value of the asset is basically a multiple of its income generating capability, as rents go up, you build equity as the value of the property goes up.

In this example, because of appreciation you would gain 20% or $14,000 of additional equity just for holding it during the time of increased rental rates—in addition to receiving all the monthly cash flow which is also increasing. *It becomes a double win— more income now plus more equity later*. Since your initial investment was only $14,000, this appreciation of the asset value is doubling your invested dollars and can have a huge impact on the total long-term return on investment. Owning capital assets enable you to profit from the effects of inflation and currency devaluation in our national economy. It's a way your personal economy can benefit even if the national economy is in turmoil.

Finally, cash flow rentals (and some other capital assets) have many other benefits relative to traditional Wall Street investment options. The rent the tenant pays is utilized to pay down the mortgage, pay for maintaining the property and pay the taxes and insurance, as well as generating cash flow passive income for you. And this income is not only taxed at lower rates than active income, but because you get to depreciate the value of the home over 27 years, it actually shelters much of the income you do receive from any taxes at all. I know many high income earning professionals who perceive substantial benefits by also having a portfolio of rental properties because of the tax sheltering advantages.

If, year after year, you build a portfolio of assets, which compound value over time and also provide sheltered income, you may be able to reinvest part of the cash flow into additional assets to reach your financial freedom point much quicker. This approach to investing almost becomes self-funding; you have created a perpetual economic engine.

Since you are dealing with inefficient markets and privately structured deals, it is possible to compound your capital at higher returns without taking on undue risk. Just think, rather than waiting

until you are in your mid 60's or 70's or beyond to "retire" → once you get out of the rat race your lifestyle choices can be much broader and more appealing—and most importantly, ***you gain back control of your time***. I know several people who started down this path early in life and became financially free by middle age. If pursued with vigor and rigor, anyone should be able to fund his or her retirement in a decade or so.

If I had understood this Plan B approach of building sustainable passive income streams through wealth pairs in my 40's, I probably wouldn't be in my early 60's still in the accumulation phase of my financial plan. As well, it would have been very helpful to already have in place significant passive cash flow before the point I lost my job/lost my active income. Unfortunately, at that point, Plan B wasn't even on my radar screen. I hadn't figured it out to protect my downside. I was just enjoying my life as a corporate executive, not really thinking about the long-term. I was left very vulnerable to someone giving me the pink slip. But now, my new strategy is clear and I am making significant progress toward my goals.

My Most Precious Asset

There are many things in life I am grateful for, but at this juncture of my life, I've discovered that I am primarily grateful for the freedom to direct my time as I choose. Time is the one thing in which we are all equal in potential. We all have 24 hours in a day. Some choose to utilize it constructively in ways that add value, creating a virtuous cycle of benefits. Others choose to expend it in ways that destroy or waste value. It's totally up to you and the decisions you make minute by minute.

When one is employed—whether in a routine role, a professional running a private practice or even in a management job you love—much of your time is not really your own. You are following the direction and/or commitments to others. When you are working, you are earning. When you are not working, you are not earning. Across my 30 year corporate career, this became a trap. My time was definitely not my own. I enjoyed what I was doing, but I was not focused on creating a secure future for my family because I was following the dictates of others.

I have learned from Michael Maloney that *"True wealth is time and freedom. Money is just a tool for trading my time. It's a container to store my economic energy until I'm ready to deploy it."* The major vision of Harder Working Money is I am attempting to set up wealth pair investments generating recurring passive income flows where my capital is working very efficiently all the time, so I don't need to. The choice is to let my money's time be leveraged and committed in specific ways to set my personal time free. This enables me to devote more time to serving others and pursuing my passions.

On my path to prosperity, as I find and execute attractive deals, I'm seeking ways to leverage my intellectual capital and relationship capital, as well as my financial capital in ways that I can do deals with others where my contributions are essential, yet not particularly time dependent. And I'm moving in the direction of continuing to remove my essential time in the business.

My desired destination is to be free to be anywhere in the world, doing whatever our hearts desire at the moment, while our money machine just keeps cranking out mailbox money in excess of our desired lifestyle burn rate. Once that occurs, we will finally be both financially free and fully flexible in our time. This seems like such a worthy goal to be pursuing.

And what are the risks in this approach? Obviously, it is dependent on our portfolio of wealth pairs to continue to generate passive income above our desired lifestyle burn rate. My perspective is that if I put myself in the position of having generated multiple streams of income initially, if some begin to peter out/experience problems, I'll just create more. If I discover that what we currently have coming in no longer meets our needs because our expenses are going up, I'll just create more. If there are new things my family decides it really wants that are outside of our budget, I'll just create more.

If I find exciting opportunities to serve others and help them achieve their goals, we'll just create more together.

It should certainly be easier to generate additional income streams once I've been successful in generating so many of them before and mastered the process/learned about pitfalls to avoid. I will clearly have the intellectual capital and relationship capital, even if we experience hiccups in financial capital. *I have discovered that, while it's great to have all three (financial / intellectual / relationship capital), if you have at least two of these bases of capital, deals can be structured and originated.*

Just to be clear, once one reaches his or her financial freedom point, it doesn't mean all value creation stops. If one chooses to work beyond this point, it's a blessing to be creating value in doing what one loves and serving the well-being of others. I hope that for several more decades I am funding deals and helping show others how to make their money work harder. But I'm hopeful that I'm doing it because I want to, not because I have to. The only thing that needs to keep working under the Harder Working Money plan is capital.

Just like pruning a bush to keep it healthy, I also envision culling my portfolio of any less desirable assets and replacing them over

time with preferred ones during my wealth maintenance phase. Moving from many smaller assets to a fewer number of larger ones → each contributes significantly more cash flow. I view this simplification of one's portfolio as a way to maximize returns while minimizing the management time required. Utilizing the 1031 exchange provisions in the tax laws, I will be able to do this by rolling my basis of the initial asset into the new one without triggering a capital gains tax event on the sale and repurchase.

Robert Kiyosaki says that wealth is a measure of time, while being rich is just a measure of your net worth on your personal financial balance sheet. This is one reason I have chosen to be more focused on creating multiple streams of income than a huge mountain of net worth. You can spend income; you can't spend assets on a balance sheet. I've decided to focus on what is essential, not the derivatives. Since I prioritize how I can choose to focus my time, I'm very focused on growing passive income wealth pairs.

Targeted Assets for Specific Purpose

Once I have covered my essential lifestyle burn rate expenses, I plan to pursue the prospect of creating additional cash flow assets targeted for a specific purpose. What I mean by this is that assets can be allocated to a certain recurring expense items in our lives. If one wants to take vacations every year that may cost $10,000, they need to acquire new assets that generate $10,000 after tax net income and only use this income stream for vacations. Set it up once and then maintain it and enjoy vacations for a lifetime.

I plan to own a sports car in the future (red Corvette convertible). I plan to pay for this car payment/insurance payment with an asset that I will acquire to cover these recurring payments. Yes, I'm willing to wait for this purchase until I find the right asset and

discover how to include it in my portfolio without diminishing the contributions of other assets. This "toy" will be an incremental automobile in my life, so I should pay for it with incremental assets. But I also realize that driving the car is just one great deal away. You might say I'm driven to achieve this specific investment milestone.

Active Investor vs. Passive Investor

A key decision each of us must select related to our investing is how active versus passive we desire to be at this time. This is peripherally true if you are focused on building a portfolio of traditional Wall Street types of securities (selecting your ideal allocation strategy and funding it appropriately) or certainly true if you are building a portfolio of alternative privately structured deals of cash flow assets.

I say "at this time" because life happens in chapters. At this time, I am very active in accumulating my portfolio of cash flow assets, as well as enhancing my relationships with people I can serve or do business with and building my knowledge base of ways to deploy capital. I'm learning to do more deals with other passive investors involved so I can help them achieve their goals, while I also progress in mine. However, as mentioned above, *I'm also building systems and structures in my business so more of it can be done without my personal involvement*. I desire to shift to a more passive role and scale my assets under management at the same time.

Participation in ownership of capital assets tends to be a team sport. Unlike a stock that you just choose to buy/sell, capital assets must be privately structured and managed. There are many roles one can choose to play. Some require significant time commitment and knowledge. Others require connections to other people who can help facilitate becoming aware of the great opportunities and

helping acquire or manage them. And finally there is the financial side. I see my role as primarily an intermediary, bringing all parties together to safely do more deals. As well, I'm a funder, deploying my capital into cash flow streams.

If you are a successful busy person who desires to allocate a portion of your financial resources into alternative investments for their superior return but limited risk, but don't want to spend the time to learn how to put these deals together by yourself, partner with others by bringing some/all of the capital to the deal. If you are an ambitious person who has studied how to do real estate or lending or building a business and can bring great deals to the table, but at this point don't have the financial capacity to take down the deal alone, look for money partners and scale the application of your deal making skills. These deals can be structured win/win for multiple parties.

If you are in a position to do it all (have the intellectual capital, the relationship capital and the financial capital), it may first appear that you can make more on each deal by doing it all yourself. While it is certainly true that you are not sharing the profits with others on each specific deal, the better question becomes *can you become involved in many more, safer deals if you choose to partner*? Can you envision a much bigger opportunity? Can you leverage what you are really good at and delegate what isn't in your wheelhouse?

Capital assets tend to be opportunities for synergy. As you will soon become aware, I own long-term hold cash flow properties with others, have LLC's to flip properties with others and am raising capital for private lending with others. I desire to transform my business with others. As I look to build my portfolio of wealth pairs, I'm actively searching for additional people to build wealth with. My thoughts are: why choose to play a smaller game when multiple people can each utilize their greatest strengths and

accomplish more together as a team? I suggest your path to prosperity will be quicker if you find a great team to play a part in.

(Note: if you would like to initiate conversations about possible opportunities for joint ventures, you can always call me at 214-682-0164, check out www.HarderWorkingMoney.com or email me at Jay@HarderWorkingMoney.com)

Chapter 5—THE MANY WEALTH BUILDING OPPORTUNITIES IN REAL ESTATE

While real estate is one of the greatest wealth builders/preservers for the affluent, there are many different entry points for investors. Learning about some of my experiences may help you select the type of investment opportunities that are most appropriate for your consideration.

Flipping for Big Paydays

Flipping generally refers to buying a property that is distressed or can be improved in some way with the intention of making it as good as new and then reselling the property as a personal residence to a new homeowner. While it isn't mandatory for the property to be physically distressed, you are very fortunate if you can acquire an asset in great condition at a significant discount to earn flipping profits. Also, while the term flipping is most often used for single family homes, it could equally apply to improving any type of distressed commercial real estate asset or business as well.

This business model typically requires buying properties at a maximum of 65% of the after repair value, less the costs of the repairs. So if a property will re-sell for $200,000 once it is fully rehabbed, and your contractor's estimate is to put $45,000 into the property to do things like replace a roof or windows, replace outdated kitchens and baths, replace worn out flooring and paint the house (as well as cover all your project carrying costs), the

most a savvy investor would pay for the property as is, is $85,000. Most will try to buy it for less because you set the table to make profits on the buy. It is a good practice to always add in a little extra contingency for added expenses because these projects rarely come in under budget.

In this example, the flipper has the potential to make about $30,000 profits, assuming they put something like $15,000 down and borrow the remaining $115,000 from a private lender. They could earn a higher total profit by not having to pay interest if they purchased and rehabbed with all cash; however, most flippers don't have the cash reserves to handle covering the full project expense out-of-pocket. This type of deal may take 4-8 months from the time the property is purchased to the time it is resold While it takes effort, and there is risk involved, it is also the chance to build up your investment capital quickly.

Just think, you risk $15,000 and have the opportunity to make double that in profit. Since the possibility is to make $30,000 in profits within six months, this translates to earning the equivalent of a 400% annual return on your invested funds. It clearly falls onto the reward scale at least at a 7-8. Many experienced flippers have multiple projects going on at one time. If you discover you have a knack for this type of activity, you can build your investment capital pot in a hurry.

But at the same time, this type of investing is also more risky than some will want to pursue. What money in this deal is most at risk? The borrower's $15,000 down payment is most at risk. The private lender will receive a 1st position mortgage on the property securing the loan. Should the borrower default, they will only have $115,000 in the deal, and have the potential to get a property worth $200,000. If they had to foreclose, they would have the possibility of selling the property for even less than it is worth to get their capital back quickly, as well as probably earn a nice return on their

money. Not only that, but even if the flipper is successful in getting the property sold, something like the first $135,000 must go to the private lender to pay off the principal and interest on the loan.

In flipping, the private lender is most secured and has legal priority to get paid back first. Then the next money made returns all closing costs such as paying the realtor his listing fee to sell the house, the title company's fees for settlement and any remaining carrying costs. And finally, after the initial $15,000 investment to the flipper, only then will the resulting profits be known.

By the same token, sometimes these houses sell for more than planned—because it's best to do all of the planning on a conservative basis. So in this case, maybe you planned that the house would sell for $200,000, and it actually sold for $210,000— so instead of making $30,000 perhaps the flipper makes $39- 40,000.

If you are an experienced flipper that knows real estate values and have a good contractor to do the project quickly and in quality fashion, the risk rating is probably a 4-5 on the 10 point scale. On the other hand, if you are a novice anxious to do your first deal, your risk may be a 9-10. I believe it is prudent for people wanting to get into flipping to do a joint venture deal with experienced rehabbers to learn the ropes from someone who can point out all the pitfalls to avoid. But at the end of the day, once you gain experience, flipping houses can be a great privately structured investment opportunity to earn big rewards with somewhat limited risk.

One negative consideration of flipping is that there are no tax advantages to this type of investment. Since one intends to hold the property less than a year, all profits are taxed at the higher earned income rate. But if you are successfully earning up to triple digits

on your money, you can afford to pay high taxes on the gain and still come out OK.

I have completed a small handful of flips and currently have 3 projects ongoing as this book is being written. I made what I expected on some of the projects and even lost money on one of them (the 1st one when I really didn't know what I was doing and experienced some difficulties with contractors). I would suggest that results in flipping can be volatile. Rehab costs go over budget and this can really eat up the profits. Timing can turn out to be longer than anticipated as you wait for the project to sell, and profitability can be over/under plan by tens of thousands of dollars. But for the right people, it is a great business model for a relatively quick profit influx of significant capital.

My current approach is that I have partnered with an experienced contractor and formed a partnership LLC to just focus on flipping. He is an expert at finding great properties and managing the rehab process. I handle the financing and resale of the property. We each take a split the profits, and I believe this the best synergistic way for me to be involved in flips. My downside risk is somewhat protected because I'm partnered with someone who has done hundreds of rehabs, and I'm leveraging his time, as well as his experience. He benefits from my business experience, capability to raise capital and put money into the deals. So we both see it as a win/win and plan to do many more of these over the next several years.

I am convinced that flipping is an important component of my current investment activities for the time being, since I am no longer a W2 employee with an active income. As well as focusing on building my long-term investment passive income streams, I also need to earn active income for current living expenses. Doing a few flips a year goes a long way toward covering this nut, as well as generates extra capital for down payments to shift into buy and

hold rental assets or short-term private lending, both of which generate cash flow.

However, once I get my passive income stream engine flowing to the point in which those activities exceed my desired lifestyle burn rate, I may limit doing as many flips on single family homes. I like this technique for a specific purpose, but at some point, I'll choose to only focus on lower risk activities that take less time commitment and may involve less drama.

Or alternatively, I may create a larger business entity to be involved with many more flips to the degree that business model may require forced appreciation. There are so many busy professionals that could greatly benefit from a portfolio of rental properties, but they neither have the time nor inclination to create these cash flow properties themselves. We are considering a business which would prepare and tenant rental properties that we could sell to this audience on an on-demand basis, related to the areas of interest and magnitude of investment this audience desires to deploy in this area.

As long as there is a great market opportunity and provided I can limit my personal time commitment, I'm not averse to having a business that can assist other passive investors earn bigger paydays as joint venture/equity partners.

Rentals for Recurring Cash Flow

The problem with flips is they are once and done. If everything works out as planned, you get the big payday but no long-term benefits. You also pay big taxes on the payday. That is why I'm also focused on building a portfolio of rental properties. I view buy and hold cash flow properties as an important foundational part of

my plan to secure my family's financial future for the long-term in ways that shelter income and are tax efficient.

Properly structured rental assets produce reliable, recurring passive income streams—they are ideal wealth pairs. Rentals shelter income, and rental income is taxed at a lower rate. The tenants pay for the upkeep of the property and pay down the mortgage balance. Rental rates tend to go up with inflation, and therefore, are a hedge against inflation/protection against the devaluation of the dollar. And finally, just like buying flip properties, you can create significant equity on the buy side, acquiring the property at a discount to the true long-term market value. Buying below true value and holding for the long-term can establish significant equity in one's rental portfolio, whether there is any annual appreciation on the value of the homes or not.

You will hear some people look down at property owners as having to deal with tenants, toilets and trash. While I have been involved in managing rentals, in the longer term, clearly my desired role is to just be a passive asset manager. I want to manage the portfolio and the management company, not be a landlord. I desire to treat rentals as a portfolio of assets no different than owning a portfolio of securities, not be involved in all the drama of the day to day operations of dealing with the tenants. One can easily do that by structuring the business with a great property management team. Yes, this means paying a 3rd party expense that reduces profitability/cash flow, but that is only really true if you place no value on your time for managing the rentals yourself. I'd rather focus my time on higher value added/less stressful activities.

A great benefit of buying rental properties is that the risk and reward of specific deals can be clearly estimated up front when evaluating which properties to buy.

The rewards on rental properties can be significant cash flow generators. Market rents are easy to discover in the area you are considering; just look up the zip code and address on www.rentometer.com, and you can see many comp rents in the immediate area. Ask a few realtors/property management companies about the overall vacancy rates in the area you are considering buying into—and run your numbers conservatively, recognizing that every year or two you may experience vacancies. Then provide your tenants with a nice place to live and treat them well, and added revenues from low turnover can be a surplus to your planned financials.

It is not uncommon for single family rentals to generate 8%+ returns on total capital just from the monthly cash flow at the start. As we will demonstrate, in the long run your returns on buy and hold cash flow properties tend to go up over time, way up in the long-term. With proper structuring and management of the process, your long-term returns on the cash you invest can be double or more the returns you start with. So certainly, the reward evaluation would at least be a 4-5 on a 10 scale initially, maybe higher depending on how good of a deal you find/the discount if any you buy it at and how you structure the financing of the deal. In the long run, that can easily be generating 6-7 on the rewards scale.

The risk side of the equation will be determined by how the asset is purchased, how your business is structured and how well the property is maintained. For example, if you start with a fully rehabbed property, repair expenses should be modest for the next several years. You should always set aside money for maintenance, so when repair bills come in, they don't need to be paid for out of current cash flow. How you finance the acquisition will also impact the deal's level of risk. If you finance it by putting down a reasonable down payment (20%+) and/or create significant equity by purchasing a distressed asset and rehabbing it before turning it

into a rental, you are mitigating financing and market valuation risks. When someone doesn't set up appropriate safeguards and systems, tries to manage or repair properties themselves and finances them with high leverage, there can be higher levels of risk. However, if you treat it like a business or a valued investment, there is no reason it can't be held to a 3-4 on a risk scale.

And a unique aspect of cash flow rentals is that, over time, as your equity builds with the tenants paying down the mortgage and rents go up because of inflation, project risk can become less and less, while your rewards go up and up. I find that this longer term → higher returns aspect very different than traditional Wall Street securities.

I don't want to understate that there can be risks in rental real estate If you are naïve on how you buy/structure the deal and how the asset is managed. I believe you get what you deserve with tenants. If properly screened, then you will be less likely to end up with tenants that trash your property, don't pay and need to be evicted, which means you will lose several months' rent (ask me how I know). But just like any business, if you build in safeguards and stay on top of the details, this business can be controlled and managed.

Important Financial Formulas to Evaluate in Rental Properties

The primary objective of building a nest egg that includes a portfolio of rental properties is to generate passive income streams of monthly cash flow. To better understand this business and compare specific deals, there are several formulas it is beneficial to comprehend. To reduce risk in real estate, you must understand the

financials of each specific property. One of my favorite sayings is, *"it all comes down to the math."*

NET OPERATING INCOME (NOI) is the total annual income generated less all the expenses related to the operation of the asset. These expenses include property taxes, insurance, property management, long-term asset maintenance, utilities (any not paid for by the tenant) and repairs.

If the tenant owes $800/month in rent, gross potential annual income should be $9,600. However, in reality, actual income could be different. Perhaps they were late on their rent one month, and you charged a $50 late fee, so your total income could be $9,650. If you experienced a month of vacancy, obviously your income would be less.

The expenses used in the NOI calculation are all expenses related to the operation of the asset, but do not include your mortgage payment if that is how you structured the purchase. Let's assume your total annual expenses are $3,400/year, or about 35% of income, which is a typical benchmark.

Total Income	$9,650.00
Total Expenses	$3,400.00
Net Operating Income (NOI)	$6,250.00

If you purchased the property with cash, your earnings on your investment would be $520/month or $6,250/year. However, most investment real estate is not owned free and clear; rather it is purchased with leverage (a mortgage). Net operating income will only be equal to cash flow if the property is owned free and clear. *The important point to realize is the profitability of the asset doesn't change whether or not you have a mortgage.*

CAPITALIZATION RATE (CAP rate) is a way of measuring how powerful an investment the asset is, meaning how much does it earn relative to the price paid. In this example, if the property was purchased at $70,000 and generates $6,250, the asset is earning 8.9% return. That is not necessarily what you are earning on your money, just the return the asset is generating.

Net Operating Income	$6,250.00
Purchase Price	$70,000.00
Capitalization Rate	8.9%

If you purchased with all cash, you are earning 8.9% on your funds. However, if you purchased with a mortgage, you will want to understand Cash on Cash Return to understand your returns after paying the mortgage expense. But to derive that, we must first understand Cash Flow.

CASH FLOW is what you earn after you pay all expenses plus the mortgage payment.

Total Income	$9,650.00
Total Expenses	$3,400.00
Net Operating Income (NOI)	$6,250.00
Mortgage	$3,600.00
Cash Flow	$2,650.00

If your mortgage is $300.00/month, this reduces your cash flow to $220.00/month or $2,650/year. Obviously, cash flow can be positive or negative. ***Great investment properties always have a decent spread between the expected total income, expenses and mortgage payment to maintain positive cash flow.***

CASH ON CASH RETURN (COCR) is a measure to evaluate how this asset performs at providing a desirable return on your invested dollars. For example, assume that you were able to buy this $70,000 rental property with 20% down and an 80% mortgage. So your cash for the down payment was $14,000, and perhaps you had another $2,000 in closing expenses. We'll assume your total out of pocket to acquire the asset was $16,000.

Cash Flow	$2,650.00
Total Dollar Investment	$16,000.00
Cash on Cash Return (COCR)	16.6%

In other words, the asset itself in this example is earning 8.9% (CAP rate). However, because of how you have structured the deal, you have almost doubled that rate of return on the money you put into the deal. ***This is an example of creating positive leverage through finance***. The reason that your rate of cash on cash return is higher is that if you are able to borrow money from the bank at 5% to buy the property, and the asset is generating 8.9%, you are gaining arbitrage (spread) on the bank's money as well as earning the full return on your own money used for the down payment.

DEBT COVERAGE RATIO (DCR) compares the net operating income of an asset related to the mortgage expense of the loan on the property, shown as a ratio.

Net Operating Income (NOI)	$6,250.00
Mortgage Expense	$3,600.00
Debt Coverage Ratio (DCR)	173%

The higher the DCR, the more your profitability and the safer your mortgage is to the lender. Most banks would want to see at least 125% DCR; however, I'm only interested if the plan calls for at least 150%. I will only consider assets with a greater spread because this is safer for me as well. The DCR is heavily influenced by how your loan is structured and the interest rates at the time you buy. For example, if mortgage interest rates were higher—say $5,000/ per year expense for the year—the net operating income of the asset wouldn't change, but the cash flow would be dramatically reduced, and you would end up with a much lower debt coverage ratio/a much riskier investment ($1,250 cash flow, 125% DCR).

LOAN CONSTANT RATE is the final formula/concept you need to understand to reduce risk in owning cash flow real estate. A loan constant measures the annual payments related to a loan. The loan constant can be dramatically different than the interest rate on a loan depending on whether the loan you select is amortizing or interest only and how long the term of the loan is.

This is a term that most investors in real estate have never heard of, yet is one of the most critical aspects of being a savvy real estate investor. Lack of understanding of loan constants has caused many investors to think they are buying a good deal, only to find out they end up with negative cash flow because of how the loan they accepted was structured. Let's be clear; you never want to own cash flow real estate that takes money out of your pocket every month!

The loan constant is the annual cash going out of your pocket, regardless of how much is principal or interest, divided by the loan amount. Our example property's monthly mortgage expense is $300/month or $3,600/year.

Mortgage Expense	$3,600.00
Amount of Loan	$56,000.00
Loan Constant Rate	6.44%

In this example, the stated annual interest rate of the loan was 5%, at 30 year amortization, on $56,000. However, the loan constant was 6.44%, which of course is higher than the stated interest rate because, in addition to paying the interest that is due each month, you are also paying an amount toward principal because it is a fully amortizing loan.

Since there can be a variety of ways to finance a property, it makes sense to evaluate different loan options before you buy. For clarity, a fully amortizing loan pays principal and interest; at the end of the loan you are fully paid off. With an interest-only loan, you are only paying the interest portion; at the end of the term you still owe back all of the principal balance.

Consider the following examples; all related to possible $56,000.00 loans on the $70,000.00 rental property we have been discussing:

	Loan 1	Loan 2	Loan 3	Loan 4
Interest Rate	4%	5%	7.5%	4.5%
Amortization	10 year term Fully amortizing	30 year term Fully amortizing	10 year Interest only	15 year Fully amortizing
Monthly payment	$566.97	$300.62	$350.00	$428.40
Loan Constant	12.15%	6.44%	7.5%	9.18%

What may surprise you in this example is that the loan with the lowest interest rate has the highest monthly payment and the

highest loan constant, because it was structured to fully pay off the loan in 10 years.

Which loan will generate the most monthly cash flow by the property? Loan #2 has the lowest loan constant of 6.44% and the lowest monthly payment of $300.62.

It is a wise practice when dealing with a bank in order to get a loan for an acquisition to ask them for a variety of ways they could finance the property. Different banks incentivize certain loan structures for internal reasons, so you can't always say that a 30 year fully amortizing loan is going to be the best deal. What matters is the rate offered relative to the amortizing term that works for your desired purpose.

Don't just look at one option; ask to see a variety of terms they can offer and then do an evaluation of how each available financing term could impact the attractiveness of the possible investment asset.

This is part of the magic of privately structured deals. *You have an element of control to be able to set things up in a way that magnifies specifically what you desire from an investment opportunity*. For personal reasons, you might want more cash flow, or you might want more principal pay down. As well as structuring to mitigate risks, you can also build in personalized advantage in the way you choose to structure every deal.

Let me clarify this point further. If you are a professional with a sizable earned income outside of real estate, you may desire to shelter income and prefer a very aggressive pay down of the rental property. In this case, loan #1 above might be your best choice. Yes, it has less cash flow in the short-term, but in 10 years, the tenant has fully paid for the loan on the property—and meanwhile you have had a larger legitimate income offset. Perhaps even a 5

year amortization period would be desirable. In an extreme case, you might even be willing to consider negative cash flow for a period of time when looking at the investment from the total perspective of your income and balance sheet benefits.

A key metric when evaluating possible deals is comparing the Capitalization Rate (what the asset is earning regardless of financing) and the loan constant (your total out of pocket expense to service the loan). In our example, we said the CAP rate was 8.9%. So loan options 2 or 3 can create *positive leverage* (loan constant is less than the CAP rate), while loan options 1 and 4 create *negative leverage* (loan constant is greater than the Cap rate). It is generally preferred to have a lower loan constant than CAP rate—to always set up the deal with positive leverage. However, just because a loan constant is higher than the CAP rate, it doesn't necessarily mean that the asset would generate negative cash flow each month, just that the financing is sub-optimally structured with negative leverage, and the deal could be improved with a different financing option. If you ever structure a deal with a loan constant > Cap rate, just be sure you are doing this for a reasonable purpose, like an intentional accelerated mortgage payoff.

Increasing Profits in Rental Real Estate

Another important point to realize is small increases in rents or to a lesser degree reductions in expenses can have a dramatic impact on the cash flow profitability of your real estate investment over time.

Study the following examples:

	Original	Increase Rents 3%	Decrease expense 3%	Both
Total Income	$9,650.00	$9,939.50	$9,650.00	$9,939.50
Total Expenses	$3,400.00	$3,400.00	$3,298.00	$3,298.00
Net Operating Income (NOI)	$6,250.00	$6,569.50	$6,352.00	$6,641.50
Mortgage	$3,600.00	$3,600.00	$3,600.00	$3,600.00
Cash Flow	$2,650.00	$2,969.50	$2,752.00	$3,041.50
Impact on Cash Flow		+12.1%	+3.9%	+14.7%

In other words, *an increase of rents of only 3% can increase your bottom line cash flow by over 12%!* This is why making sure over time you continually keep rents current to what the market will bear (and charging your tenants late fees if they don't pay you on time) can dramatically impact your investment's performance. Small annual bumps to the rental rate and charging late fees can accumulate to huge increases in your monthly take, over time.

Similarly, look to decrease your expenses when feasible. Now I'm not talking about neglecting maintenance issues, just eliminating inefficiencies. Sometimes preventative maintenance is critical to reducing ongoing expenses. You can also buy supplies in bulk. The other thing is making sure you charge back the tenants for problems they caused, rather than eating the expense. You need to train your tenants that they are responsible for the damage they cause from neglect. And finally, when appropriate, appeal the taxes on your property. This can be a major expense item, and small setbacks of the taxes will drop straight to your bottom line.

As can be seen, changes in income have more impact on profits than reducing expenses on a percentage basis. If you were successful in increasing rents 3% and reducing expenses 3%, your cash flow would increase an amazing 14.7%! Realize this increase is totally due to better management of the asset, no incremental investment capital was required.

One of the reasons long-term holds on cash flow real estate can be a great investment is that since *rents tend to go up over time with inflation, yet your major cost to cash flow is a mortgage payment that can be fixed, in time your cash flow can grow exponentially.*

	Original	10 year rental growth
Total Income	$9,650.00	$12,000.00
Total Expenses	$3,400.00	$4,228.00
Net Operating Income (NOI)	$6,250.00	$7,772.00
Mortgage	$3,600.00	$3,600.00
Cash Flow	$2,650.00	$4,172.00
Impact on Cash Flow		+57.4%

In this example, I also increased expenses the same proportion as the rents went up; however, typically you can hold these to a lesser growth rate. But even without holding down expense growth, the profitability of your investment went up over 57% just because of inflationary impact on rents over the long run.

Finally, there is the consideration of possible appreciation of the asset. If you believe that it is likely we will experience significant inflation over time, particularly because our government continues to print and print more money deflating its value, it is very

beneficial to own hard assets, which protect value over time. Cash flow rental properties are one such example…stocks not so much.

I believe we are in a long-term inflationary situation, and this is one key reason I'd rather own a portfolio of cash flow properties than a portfolio of stocks and bonds. Real estate has utility value, and in times of inflation, rents go up. Inflation also causes the value of the property to go up, as well. In time, a portfolio of properties that you invested hundreds of thousands of dollars in can become worth millions because of the appreciation of hard assets as our dollars devalue.

I hope through all of these formulas you begin to experience how owning capital assets can be very beneficial relative to Wall Street securities. Because you have the opportunity to structure the deal for specific advantage, it can deliver more desirable results for your specific situation. With stocks/mutual funds, you buy them in hope that in the long term they consistently compound as our overall economy grows. That type of investing is based on speculation. However, with capital assets, you are deciphering the math of specific opportunities and setting them up for a favorable financing opportunity to generate reliable streams of cash flow. Over the long-term as you hold cash flow assets they typically become safer and tend to generate more profits.

Scaling Returns With Commercial Real Estate

Most people who own rental real estate start off with single family homes or small multi-family homes like duplexes, triplexes or quads (2, 3 or 4 unit small apartments). This seems to be the most affordable point of entry into cash flow real estate and is a good place to cut one's teeth into something new. I am aware of many real estate investors who just continue to build a large portfolio of

single family rental properties for their long-term plan for cash flow during retirement. They often are not managing the assets, but just tend to like holding on to their ever-growing portfolio. There is certainly nothing wrong with this incremental approach of owning a portfolio only containing single family homes.

However, one of my key strategies is to always be *looking for how to be more efficient and to scale results*. I figure if one plans to get to 50 doors or 500, why try to reach that goal with a bunch of small acquisitions, when there are definite efficiencies of larger properties?

I also know some people with big dreams who try to step straight into large $7-10,000,000, one hundred plus unit apartment complexes as a first step in real estate. Some have partnered into these deals successfully, but most big dreamers do a lot of work trying to find an asset they have no realistic expectation of landing. I figure if you only have experience with a small fishing pole, it's kind of stupid to think you can go fishing for Moby Dick.

I've chosen to move my way upstream with more of a Goldilocks approach. My first multi-family is a 6-plex small apartment that I acquired with a partner. It's a great performing asset, and I'd like to own a dozen more just like it. Our cash on cash return on it varies from the mid-teens and higher, and our long-term results will be over 30% return on investment because of the sizable equity we created on the buy. I'm constantly reviewing opportunities to acquire other small, multi-families like this one, but I realize finding an asset this good is like finding a needle in a haystack.

About a year ago, a couple of other investors and I purchased a 34 unit apartment complex as my next progression in a "just right size" asset to add to my portfolio. It's a nice class C complex in an area of good blue collar workers, and we have a part-time onsite

manager. Having on-site representation makes a lot of difference in reducing the risk and lightening our load. While this asset doesn't meet the exceptional returns of my 6-plex, once again it's turned out to be a solid performer because we did a thorough job of due diligence to understand the pros and cons of this asset before we purchased it. We have already addressed a many of the opportunities for improvement/deferred maintenance issues, and the property is in much better shape today than when we purchased it. This implies our equity position has already grown. And importantly, we are gaining experience with larger properties, which should aid us in stepping further up-market when an appropriate and even larger deal comes along.

From a risk and reward standpoint, I believe *there is a clear reduction in risk moving from single family homes to multi-family properties*. This comes from the impact of a vacancy. In our 34 unit property, even if we have turnover of 3 tenants in a month (much higher than we are experiencing), it would represent less than a 10% reduction in our monthly income. With a single family property, if you lose your tenant, and it takes 2 months to get a replacement, it can reduce your <u>annual</u> income by over 16%! And the expenses/mortgage payments don't stop just because you don't have a tenant in the home. Because of this differential, while I position single family homes as a cash flow real estate investment as a 3-4 on the risk scale, I place multi-family as a lower 2-3 risk type of asset.

How about the rewards? Obviously, you add at least one zero to the end of every number, but at the end of the day, rents on apartments tend to be slightly less than for a single family home. This is because 2-3 bedroom houses will tend to be larger than corresponding 2-3 bedroom apartments, and given their choice, many people prefer to be living in a home versus an apartment. However, this difference in rents tends to be offset by efficiencies

in expenses of running the investment properties. So overall, from a cash flow standpoint, they are similar.

At the end of the day, when comparing single family homes or apartments, the possible returns on specific assets tend to be more offset by the specifics of the deal than the tendencies of one asset class to be better than the other. If you are smart in your acquisitions and efficient in your management, I believe either single family houses or multi-family apartments can predictably earn at least 8%+ COCR in the short-term and up to double that in the long-term. In my book, this would equate to a 4-5 on the returns scale at the buy and 5-6 in the long-term. Once again, with any type of rental property, it is possible to structure deals with higher rewards relative to the risk taken.

In full disclosure, I have experience one major misstep in commercial cash flow real estate. A partner and I purchased a 33 pad distressed mobile home community that was over 1,000 miles from Philly. Do you sense where this is going? We thought we had good management in place and a turnaround plan to improve the business into a strong cash flow performer. However, there were definitely lessons to learn. It started off negatively, and went downhill from there.

If you are buying a strong cash flowing asset with good management in place, distance probably shouldn't be an issue. After all, you often need to go where the great opportunities are in commercial real estate, rather than assuming you can find great deals in your back yard. It is a numbers game. You can always find lots of rental houses in any market (although some markets create much higher cash flow than others, depending on property values and rental rates); however, locating great multi-family deals is much tougher work because there are few available at one time. Great deals have great financials, and perhaps the financials of local deals may not be appealing to savvy investors. So in larger

commercial real estate investing, keep looking and reach for the special opportunities wherever you can find them, even out of your home town.

However, if the deal has hair on it, and you need substantial change to improve the financials, we've learned turnarounds require more personal involvement than is possible at a distance. Needless to say, we no longer own that property, and yes, there were significant losses involved. But we also gained lessons that we will utilize for decades to come. Sometimes failure is a part of learning how to grow and do better deals.

I will add that mobile home communities can be great assets for generating substantial cash flow. Mobile homes are the most affordable home sector, and there is substantial need for this class of housing. My father developed a 122 space community and ran it for 25 years. Now my brother is running it, and the cash flow just keeps on coming every month. Almost one million dollars of equity has been created since this asset was purchased. It has been a great long-term investment for my extended family.

I have grand ambitions for significant passive income streams with larger multi-family apartments or other commercial cash flow real estate, but I won't dwell on that here. After all, they are only dreams, and I'm attempting primarily to share my experiences and insights for your benefit.

Finally, I will add that I believe commercial real estate is definitely a team sport. In my opinion, one should not attempt to do these larger deals alone. Partner with people who have skills and experiences that can be leveraged to lead you to grander destinations with more security along the journey. This also shares any possible risk with other partners, and I judge this to be an effective risk mitigation technique of involvement in larger asset acquisitions.

Apartment deals can be great opportunities for passive investment partners. Team up with someone who has good education and experience, and you will likely be involved with a relatively low risk investment and attractive rewards.

Beyond Cash Flow—Real Estate Is Great For Building Long-term Equity

There is a huge difference in building equity in traditional stocks/mutual funds and building equity in real estate.

In the stock and bond model of building a large equity balance, you initially put the capital you want to invest toward buying assets, and then you typically continue to add contributions each month or quarter to build your account value. If the values on these assets go up, net of all the fees charged, and if there are dividends and you continue to reinvest this extra money, your account value will build faster. As previously discussed, in the Wall Street model you typically require decades of compounding to achieve your targeted portfolio value. And because this Wall Street asset model depends on building mountains of equity to be in a position to distribute value over your retirement years as income, it is essential to build huge equity balances in your portfolio, or you may outlive your account balance.

With cash flow real estate, you typically put a small portion of the purchase price of the acquisition in at purchase, and fund the rest with leverage (a mortgage). The first major opportunity to build equity in real estate is buying the asset under its full market value. This can be done either buy buying distressed assets and creating value as you improve it, or by just locating motivated sellers. It is not uncommon to be able to create 15-35% equity on the buy,

which will often amount to many thousands of dollars. Then, over time, there are three additional opportunities to grow your equity:

1. A portion of the income from the rentals goes to paying down the mortgage balance, and this increases your equity every month. As we previously discussed, the payment that goes toward principal is modest in the early years, but over time, becomes significant. If you hold the single family home property we've been using as an example until the end of the mortgage, you only put $14,000 as a down payment. Over the years, the tenant's rent will go to paying off the other $56,000 mortgage balance. (This is key: with cash flow investment properties the asset is paying for itself rather than requiring additional cash to pay down the mortgage.) As your mortgage payoff balance goes down, your equity position goes up.

2. In our example, after all expenses and the mortgage payment, you would initially net about $220 cash flow. Because this is sheltered income (depreciation on the asset will shelter close to $200/month in income), you will not generally owe taxes on this income. If you need this cash flow for other purposes, it will be spent and not add value. However, if you accumulate at least part this income and reinvest, just as in the stock/bond example above of reinvesting dividends, it can help you buy more assets quicker to build your total portfolio value in a much shorter period of time. More assets generally imply more equity.

3. For the reasons we've explained earlier in this book, over time, the value of the dollar goes down and the value of hard assets goes up. This shows up in two places. First, over time, your rental income will tend to grow. Second, the value of your property also tends to appreciate, which builds equity. Each of these shifts reduces the risk of owning the asset over time.

The combined effect of all of these factors can multiply the equity growth of your real estate portfolio at much higher rates than is in common of Wall Street equities, net of fees. But a key differentiator is that *building equity in a real estate portfolio is typically serendipity, not the point of the investment*. When accumulating a portfolio of cash flow investment properties, what you are primarily after is the monthly cash flow, not building equity. You intend to hold the assets for the long-term, not sell them for income. Building equity can accelerate your investment results because, once you have substantial equity, you can refinance it to monetize the equity and buy additional cash flow assets. Over time, your portfolio continues to grow based on its own performance.

Playing Monopoly in Real Life

The more I ponder my next steps investing in real estate, I comprehend that it is like playing the board game Monopoly in real life. First, you get into the game earning cash flow buying properties and adding rental houses. You work your way around the board accumulating attractive assets whenever possible. Sometimes you flip one asset to another player to get a different one that makes more sense for your portfolio. As your portfolio grows, you comprehend the added value of scaling and three green houses turns into one red hotel.

In real life, it becomes a game about building more and more streams of passive income, and in the long run, gaining substantial equity as mortgages are paid down and the possibility for appreciation in asset values grow. If you don't have capital for down payments, you may need to occasionally flip properties to generate profits, so you can transition this profit into buy and hold properties.

As with all privately structured investment deals in an inefficient market, you need to evaluate the pros and cons of each individual asset for unique characteristics that make a compelling opportunity. It's not as simple as deciding you like Apple computers or iPhones and believe the brand will continue to grow in value, so you want to own Apple stock.

With real estate, you are attempting to sort through all the rocks and find the diamonds or gold. *This often means you are wise to team together with people very experienced in the game*. But one thing that can't be questioned is if real estate is a viable investment sector. It's been proven, over the decades, substantial cash flow and wealth can be accumulated by providing a nice place for people to live. Regardless of what happens in our overall economy, there will always be an ever-growing need for good housing. While many other market sectors can decline very significantly in value during a troubled economy, there will always be significant utility value in residential real estate.

This is a Great Time for Real Estate

In summary, *one of the strong appeals of buying cash flow real estate today is that current conditions are perfect for enhanced cash flow*. There is strong demand for rental properties, especially by the large Millennial generation pushing up rents and lowering vacancy rates. The prices of real estate are lower today than they were a few years ago in the real estate bubble, which reduces your overall investment level and raises the prospect of possible appreciation. Certainly, the interest rates are at historical lows, allowing you many options to structure the deal for a desired blend of cash flow and equity appreciation, as well as higher levels of cash flow than have historically been the case. I believe the combination of increased rental rates, lower purchase prices and

cheaper money makes this is a perfect opportunity to build a portfolio of rentals for strong passive income streams over the long run.

In other words, today there is an excellent opportunity in real estate for savvy investors to transition investment capital out of volatile Wall Street securities and into Harder Working Money cash flow assets.

Don't Forget; It's a Financing Game

I am an advocate of real estate as an important element of my financial plan. But I want to be clear; *building wealth through real estate is not about the houses or apartments* → *it's about the financing opportunity*. The primary reason houses and apartments are appealing to me is they can be used as collateral to borrow money, so I can create spreads and earn either cash flow income streams for the long run (rentals) or forced appreciation in the short run (flipping). If I could just as easily and reliably do the same thing with sports cars—I'd rather be in the sports car business. I find cars emotionally appealing, while houses and apartments don't turn me on. It's the cash flow and the capital accumulation that are possible with real estate that I'm interested in, and they possibly represent an opportunity for you as well.

Chapter 6—ENJOY THE BANKER'S BENEFITS THROUGH PRIVATE LENDING

By far the safest/most secure place to be involved in real estate is with your name (entity) on the Mortgage (Deed of Trust in some states) *as the lender*. In this way, you are participating in the real estate market's profit opportunities, without the risks associated with personally owning the property.

Overall, the benefits of short-term private lending on investment properties include generating high stated rate returns with limited downside risk because the funding is secured by properties with a big cushion of equity. The banker's benefit is they are always the FIRST TO EARN AND LAST TO LOSE.

As I previously discussed in the chapter on investing and using the buckets model, your investment portfolio should include both growth oriented assets, as well as other more conservative wealth preservation, income oriented assets. I view private lending as a fantastic opportunity to have substantial capital deployed in income generating assets in ways that are inherently less risky than owning properties. I characterize private mortgage lending as conservative assets in my investment bucket because of the lower volatility and risk. And yet, private lending returns can rival the high returns of some of the riskiest high growth oriented Wall Street securities. Short of tax benefits (which lending really doesn't generate other than a great place to use self-directed IRA funds), *I judge private lending to be the best way to generate huge spreads in return versus risk in all of the asset classes in my portfolio of privately structured deals.* I currently maintain a sizable portfolio

of private mortgages I'm participating in and plan to do so indefinitely.

What is private lending? It is where private individuals/companies make loans to other individuals/small businesses just like the banks do; however, the money that is being lent, and the underwriters of the loans are individuals instead of institutions. These loans are closed through a title company and have title insurance just like a loan from Bank of America. But rather than coming from a federally chartered bank, private lending is just individuals lending to other individuals for mutual economic benefit.

In the broadest terms, there are two types of loans. Secured loans have a mortgage on a property, which provides protection of the lender's capital in case the borrower defaults. Unsecured lending is much riskier because, while the borrower promises to pay it back, if he defaults, the lender doesn't go seize assets. Think of unsecured lending like a credit card. If you go buy a nice dress and put it on your credit card, and then don't make the required payments, the credit card company won't come to your house and take away your clothes. They will go after you for the debt owed, but it isn't tied to any specific thing. With secured lending, if our borrowers don't pay, we will take ownership of the house that is securing the loan. *I believe short-term loans backed by mortgages on investment properties are the safest type of lending there is, provided the cushion of protective equity is substantial*.

My lending focus is being the private banker to experienced real estate investors. My current loans are all short-term in nature, often 6-9 month terms. I'm funding two types of deals. The majority of my loans are to people flipping homes; loans are for both the acquisition and rehab, with high interest rates and huge cushions of protective equity. I also have loans to investors who want to buy/hold cash flow rental properties. But with these, I'm just an interim funding solution to these borrowers. Often the banks won't

lend on distressed properties, and these borrower's business model is often to buy distressed property at a sizable discount, fix it up to be a great rental property, put a tenant in it and then go to the bank for long-term financing on an income producing asset. My short-term interest rates are fine for the fix up stage, but are far too expensive for the holding phase of cash flow rentals.

To obtain my interim short-term loan, the borrowers need to provide a down payment for the initial loan (I want them to put skin in the game); however, often they increase the value of the property so much by fixing it up that they can often fully pay off our loan with a take-out loan through a traditional bank and end up with little or no cash in the deal in the long run. They have created their equity by fixing up a distressed asset and turning it into a cash flow property. This means they end up with a HUGE cash on cash return, as well as very strong cash flow streams each month. They achieved this by using their intellectual and relationship capital more than their financial capital. And of course, we as lenders receive a great return for the short-term use of our money that enables the deal to be done/the value to be created.

You might be wondering, "I've heard of the banks taking back all of these homes in foreclosures when the economy crashed in 2008…isn't being the bank and lending risky?" I say it depends on the specifics and how you structure the deal. I certainly have no interest in being a lender to homeowners on their primary residence, with 30 year loans like the FHA makes, which are at very low rates (4-5%) and where the homeowner only puts down 3-4% down payment. Similarly, I won't even to entertain conventional loans to homeowners with a 20% down payment/80% loan to value and similar low rates. No, our type of lending will require a maximum 70% loan to value (often less) for more equity protection, and loans *are only made to borrowers on investment properties where the deals can support interest rates that are very*

high (double digits) and there is a plan to pay us back in the next six to nine months.

Why would investors be willing to pay us such high rates? Because they look at the cost of money as just another cost of being able to fix up the property. Paying someone $15,000 for the short-term use of money is no different than paying $15,000 for a new kitchen and refurbished baths in the house. The deal either makes economic sense considering all the costs, or it does not. As previously discussed, there are huge profit opportunities in real estate today, and this enables our borrowers to afford to pay a high interest rate and still have a very attractive deal.

I think it's kind of funny. The banks won't lend to the investors on short-term loans improving distressed properties where there is huge creation of value. We love these loans. However, banks are happy to lend 30-50% more on a property than we would, accept far less down payment and charge one-third the rate or less interest. And they think our loans are risky?

Of course, it's the bank's lack of interest in lending on distressed properties which creates opportunity for private lenders. If banks started offering loans to our prospective borrowers at 5-7% interest, much of the private lending market would dry up and wither away. But as long as these types of very lucrative, very safe loans exist, I will likely be keeping a significant portion of my money in short-term private mortgages because I perceive them to be high yield conservative investments.

The 3 Tasks of Lenders

In order to be an effective private lender, there really are only three key tasks the loan originator needs to master:

1. Find qualified borrowers who have demonstrated experience/specialized skills to turn capital into much more capital in a short period.
2. Find sources of money to lend out, at a rate lower than the borrower is willing to pay.
3. Structure safer and profitable loans, using appropriate mitigation techniques to shift most of the risk to the borrower, so the money partner's funds are protected.

Just like the banks, lenders often lend out money that isn't their own. By creating an opportunity supported by a mortgage and promissory note that someone is willing to fund (because the funder feels the specifics of the deal are a great investment) in essence, the lender is creating an asset (the loan) that generates cash flow out of thin air. Unlike the borrower, the lender doesn't need to buy a property to generate the cash flow. Lenders don't need to deal with property repairs or cost overruns. The asset on the lender's balance sheet is the loan that he created. This asset is offset by the liability of having to pay back the funder for the use of their money. This loan will create cash flow for the lender and the person who puts up the money to fund the deal, as stated in the terms of their agreement.

It truly is a win/win/win scenario:

- The borrower wins because he or she has access to the capital needed to buy/fix up the property and generate substantial value which greatly exceeds the cost of the capital.

- The funder wins because he or she has a high interest rate/cash flow opportunity with low risk and because the loan is secured by a property worth much more than is being lent.
- The loan originator wins by lending money that isn't his at a rate that is higher than he is paying the funder, leveraging his intellectual and relationship capital to originate and manage the deal.

Of course there is no reason the funder and the loan originator cannot be the same person.

A key point about mastery of lending is that it should be driven by safety. When one qualifies the borrower's prior experience at fixing up properties and paying back loans, and all the numbers of the deal are conservative, the loan is safer. When one sets up the rules so the loan is made to a low loan to value of the property, and the property is in a decent neighborhood, the loan is safer. When the borrower puts up a significant down payment or other collateral, the loan is safer. If the loan is set up with monthly interest payments, and these are impounded in escrow from the time the loan was originated, the loan is safer. If there is a rehab budget, and these funds are held in escrow until inspections demonstrate that the property has been improved, the loan is safer. Safer loans are possible if you design them to be so and then follow the rules you set up. Such is the benefit of privately structured deals where the returns can be magnified and the downside risk can be limited.

To the degree that investing typically involves some speculation (betting on an uncertain outcome), lending is more of a financing strategy than an investing strategy. All factors of the deal will be evaluated before the loan is offered. The terms of the loan are clearly established up front—there is a stated rate of return. There is no question about the terms of payback; they are

clearly included in all the legal documents. There is no question about what qualifies as default; all of the obligations of the borrower are also clearly stated. *Safety and control is one of the main reasons that I perceive private mortgage lending to be a very conservative investment strategy*.

The Benefits of Lending Versus Owning Properties

Both private lending and purchasing investment properties can be great investments for different reasons. I'm committed to doing many more of each of these types of investments as I continue to build my passive income retirement nest egg.

However, I certainly perceive owning properties to be the riskier of the two. And while, in the long-term, one can accrue many benefits in flipping properties or owing cash flow rental properties discussed elsewhere in this book, there are also many benefits on the lending side of the ledger. Most of these benefits relate to reducing risks to the lender by establishing the rules that shift risks to the borrower.

Private Lender	Property Owner/Borrower
Defines the rules for a loan he is willing to make	Provides all of the information to qualify for the loan and must follow the rules offered
Decides if it's a good deal/offers the terms unique to a specific deal/borrower	Can either accept or reject what is offered
Lawyers create all the legal paperwork in the advantage of the lender.	Signs a confession of judgment and personal guarantee and pays for the legal documents
No costs to establish a loan	Pays the down payment and closing costs

Named as loss payee on property insurance and title insurance	Pays for the property insurance and title insurance
Controls the rehab funding in escrow, to only be released as the property is improved	Does all the work to the property, if there are over runs must be paid by the borrower
Less risk: fixed terms and protective equity	More risk: down payment money at most risk, must create the value for profits beyond paying off lender and getting his down payment back
Gets paid first	Gets paid last
Laws protect lenders capital, last to lose	Foreclosure if default, first to lose
Shielded from litigation on the property	Exposed to liability of the property

As I say, the sides are different. One is riskier, has more upside potential and tax benefits. The other is safer and still gets a lucrative stated return. At this moment, I have a number of loans where I am the lender and a few loans where I am the borrower. I obviously feel all of these loans are beneficial, or I wouldn't have signed my name to them. But each satisfies different financial objectives that I am seeking in my real estate investments and overarching financial plan.

Funding Private Lending Deals...and Opportunities to Participate

While I started this chapter off saying that private lending requires private capital, that doesn't necessarily mean that all of the money is from the person who knows how to find the experienced / qualified borrowers, vet the property and the borrower, negotiate

and close the deal, manage the rehab deal and then be at the payoff when the loan pays out.

My business model is to generally put some of my own money into every loan I originate. Sometimes I fund an entire small loan myself. However, I come across many more great deals than I have funds to put into loans. *To be in a position to fund more deals, I also allow people I know with capital who desire to participate in private loans to join in as funding partners in these deals*. We often structure these as fractional participation so we each have a stated share of the loan. There is always a small spread between what the borrower is willing to pay and what I pass on to my funding partners. This compensates me for finding, putting together and managing the loan.

Once the local real estate community became aware that I was lending, I got calls every week from prospective borrowers. Certainly, most of the people I talk to will probably never become one of my borrowers. Perhaps they don't have enough experience or sufficient cash to bring to the table. Sometimes we don't see eye to eye on how business should be done—safely and securely for the lender. That is one of the nice things about being a lender—you set the rules that make sense to you. If the borrower doesn't like your rules, they can go find someone else to lend them money.

Many times it's the deal I'm evaluating that turns out to not be such a great deal. That is a fantastic thing about being a lender. I have so many deals coming across my desk. I get to see deals of all types. I see deals where the borrowers attempt to fudge the numbers to try to make it look like a good deal, and this teaches me something about the integrity of the prospective borrower. I also see fantastic deals that I wish were my own. As well I get to see so many contactors' quality of workmanship that I'm developing more expertise in what attributes I think make a great property for re-sale.

As the lender, you will only lend when everything meets your criteria. That is true whether you are the loan originator or just a passive funder in the deal. You choose where your money goes in deals that meet your personal criteria. You have more control with privately structured deals.

Now, I'll be the first to admit that I've made mistakes as a lender with borrowers I wish I'd said no to. Some started out great, but when issues arose, they didn't handle their side of the equation well. Others, I didn't do sufficient due diligence to learn all the specifics of the deal or the character of the individual. Experience can be a good teacher.

This is one reason it is preferred to get involved in private lending, initially, with people who have initiated a number of loans and have a higher level of experience. I'm a different lender today than I was a few years ago because I've originated over 35 loans and have been through several good ones and several one's where we needed to problem solve. It is an effective risk mitigation technique to leverage the experience and insights of people who have become good at what you desire to do. Then if in time you decide to originate your own loans, you will have the benefit of experience on a number of loans you participated in.

But the overall point I'm trying to make is that *experienced lenders get lots of demand for loans, so most are always looking for passive participants with capital to help enable them to make more loans.* You may need to sort around through the private lenders to find people with the same attitude about safety and proper deal structuring as you have. One nice thing about the funding side is that while you need the loan originator to be local, funders can come from anywhere in the world. I believe private lending on investment properties is a great place to become a passive partner in lucrative, lower risk deals.

I'm always looking for new funding partners because I desire to take advantage of every great loan from a great borrower that comes across my desk. I hate to pass them by just because all of our available money is out. That just represents a missed opportunity to serve more people.

The Bankers Code Platinum Community

Since 2011 I have been a proud member of the preeminent private lending community in the US, George Antone's Bankers Code Platinum Community. This group now includes over 350 experienced private lenders all across the US. We work together in many ways to ensure we are all growing independent businesses while leveraging each other's successes. There are literally thousands of loans available for joint participation each year.

I have started putting personal funds into other Platinum Community deals. The simple truth is in real estate some markets are hotter than others. While I've had success in the Philadelphia market, some markets have quicker resale than we do here and private lending is a velocity of money business. I need to protect my business in case my local business dries up for one reason or another. It is so helpful to have Platinum Community members sponsoring deals all across the country.

Having the opportunity to participate in nationwide deals within this community is very beneficial to my funding partners too. Now whenever people have funds to deploy, they don't need to wait until I sponsor my next deal. Getting money invested right away is a key efficiency technique to maximize returns.

Summary of Private Lending

I don't want the perception to be that even though I stated I perceive lending to be a conservative and safer investment that there is no risk. That is certainly not the case. It is just that, in privately originated loans, the lender can structure the deal to possibly mitigate some risks and shift others to the borrowers. Every private lender will have different approaches and qualifications for their loans, and you will want to discuss the details if you choose to partner in other lender's deals.

But risks can be reduced and shifted. If you have a proper perception of the value of the collateral when fixed up, and if the quality of the fix up is good, the huge cushion of equity is there to protect the lender. If the character of the people you choose to do business with is high, everyone can work together to overcome obstacles that pop up. Just realize we are dealing with people. Sometimes people do stupid things. Sometimes there is neglect. Some people are just evil. I hope you never get involved with evil/irresponsible people because it always turns out ugly.

There is risk in everything you do. I believe when you are dealing with investment or financing opportunities where you can learn about and check all the facts—understand how value will be created and how it will be shared among the parties—then lending is a relatively safe opportunity with far greater returns possible than risks that need to be accepted.

I believe that passive participation in short term private mortgages on investment properties is a perfect way to deploy self-directed IRA funds. What a better way to compound your retirement account funds at a relatively high return in a tax advantaged environment. And it's all done without fees to the funder.

If you discover that private lending works for you, it can also be very beneficial in the long run when you are taking distributions from your retirement account. Because it is safely generating high returns, you are less likely to be depleting your capital base as you fund your desired lifestyle expenses.

Chapter 7—WEALTH PRESERVATION STRATEGIES OF THE AFFLUENT

There are two distinctly different tasks related to wealth & prosperity: creating it and sustaining it. One only has to look at the litany of professional athletes, lottery winners and 2nd/3rd generation affluent to realize that creating/having wealth at one time can be very different than learning to preserve and nurture the goose that laid the golden egg. I believe when you generate wealth on the basis of intellectual and relationship capital as well as financial capital, it is less risky because you understand how the deals generate profits.

Let's be clear, I'm not necessarily talking about the accumulation and distribution phases of funding retirement. The wealth preservation strategies and techniques I'm discussing here have application in all stages of one's life, but they do presume that you have at least a small amount of investable capital to start with and ongoing funding resources beyond your current lifestyle burn rate. Consider these an adjunct or possible replacement to the strategies targeted to fund of your retirement.

The concepts that follow are little known tools that the affluent have used for generations to preserve and continue to grow their vast wealth. I believe these same tools can have application to any bold and ambitious person who desires to leverage his or her capital with powerful financial strategies, which can enhance lifestyles. I believe these strategies can transform the money that flows through people's lives into Harder Working Money.

The Family Bank

The concept of a Family Bank is a simple principle. It was first practiced in 1760 by a German named Mayer Rothschild who controlled the way his 5 sons could access the family's vast fortune, so it would sustain into perpetuity. His Family Banking concept created the greatest financial dynasty the world had ever known. Hundreds of years later, it has provided significant financial benefit for the many Rothschild family descendants, as their wealth continues to grow and grow.

As used in the context of this book, *the purpose of a Family Bank is to be able to recapture interest that you are currently paying others for your long-term benefit, as well as to stack financial benefits in the long-term once your Family Bank has access to excess capital.* As I utilize the term *stacking benefits, it means using money in more than one way, each way contributing something positive in liquidity, cash flow or compounding.*

Virtually every person uses credit of some sort today, and when assessing most family's budgets it is observed that as much as one-third of all after tax income is going toward interest paid to 3rd parties. Home mortgages, car loans, credit card balances, student loans—the list goes on and on. So much of one's cash flow being spent on interest can be a huge detriment in the ability to save and invest for retirement. If you are able to recapture some of the interest currently going to others, you can accumulate more and more capital over time without having to earn any more income, as your Family Bank self-funds in small increments of recaptured interest.

How Private Banking Works

A Family Bank can be structured in simple to complex structures. Let's start simple.

Let's presume you are currently carrying $15,000 of debt on your Visa card, and while you try to make more significant payments, you often only are able to make the minimum monthly payment. If you study the details of your credit card, you will likely find that you are paying between 16-20% interest on your carryover balance. Clearly it will take you a long time to pay off this debt under your current practices, and the interest charges collected by others are significant.

Furthermore, let's assume that you are going to get a tax refund (or some other influx of cash) of $5,000.00 this year. Rather than just decide to spend that on something for immediate gratification or responsibly send it in to Visa, you decide to start your Family Bank as I'm advocating.

So you go to your local bank and open a new account that you call The Leigeber Family Bank, or whatever else you'd like to call your account. You deposit the $5,000 into this account. Then you, as the owner of the bank, decide you are going to make a loan to pay off $5,000 of your credit card balance. You should document the loan with a promissory note and loan repayment schedule at the same rate of interest you were paying the credit card company. It's a great learning opportunity to get your whole family together and discuss how the family now has a bank and is going to make a loan. You can discuss how paying interest is a big family expense, and now you are taking responsible action to control it for the family's long-term benefit. Sign the documents, and send in the $5,000 payment to the credit card company.

At this point, your total debt and cash flow situation hasn't changed. You still owe $15,000 in total, and your monthly payments can still be the same. They are now just split into owing it to two different creditors. $10,000 is owed to Visa, and their monthly minimum payment is now less because you have less of a balance. The other $5,000 is owed to your Family Bank, and the minimum payment is the difference of what you would have paid Visa. When you pay back your Family Bank on the $5,000 loan, you will recapture $800 or more that would have gone to Visa, plus get back the $5,000 principal. In essence, *you have turned your tax refund into investment capital*, rather than spending it on lifestyle expenses.

I like to think of this from the standpoint that *interest recaptured is the same as interest earned. Where else can you get the opportunity to earn 16% safely and securely on your funds?* And since you are the owner of the bank, if along the way the terms of the loan need to be modified, it isn't something that will ding your credit or cause a judgment. On the other hand, when you have opportunities to pay back more than the monthly minimum, continue to pay the minimum to Visa and put the extra in your Family Bank, so you are maintaining more flexibility and control of your liquidity.

Now comes the part where you really begin to benefit. Let's say you get to the point that you have accumulated $2,000 in your Family Bank from the monthly payments. It's time for another new loan. Perhaps, at this point, you still owe Visa $10,000, so now you can reduce it to $8,000. Your minimum monthly payment to Visa will go down, but your minimum monthly payment to your Family Bank will not go up because you are now paying off less total debt.

Keep up this cycle of accumulate and pay down, and you should be able to pay off the entire debt earlier—while capturing a significant amount of the interest plus principal, which would have been gone

forever—and you have accomplished this without increasing your monthly expenses.

Over time, as you fully pay off the $15,000 total debt that had been on your Visa card, your Family Bank will eventually recapture $2,400+ interest + $15,000 principal on just this first debt you erase. This is money that would have been lost to you but now is an asset for future compounding/reducing future interest going to others.

A More Complex Family Bank Example

Now let's get a bit more complicated and start to accrue more significant benefits quicker.

Presume the same starting point of a $15,000 Visa Debt, and you decide to tap into some of the equity in your home. Assume you have $40,000 equity in your home and could qualify to get a $20,000 Home Equity Line of Credit at 3% interest. You set up the line of credit and use it to start your Family Bank. Next, you create a new loan, tapping your HELOC to pay off your Visa bill in full. So $15,000 goes into your bank from the HELOC with a 3% interest charge, and you lend yourself $15,000 to pay off Visa at 16%. Every month, you make the same payment that you would have made to Visa, but instead it goes into your Family Bank, and a small portion goes from your Family Bank to pay interest on the HELOC.

As you pay off this debt over time, you will recapture $2,400+ that you would have paid Visa. But your Family Bank also paid $450 in interest payments to your lender on the HELOC. The point of going through all of this is you have been able to not change a penny going out of your pocket on a monthly basis, but over time can recapture $1,950+ in interest. This is basically the arbitrage of

using the equity in your home, which you can borrow at a low rate, to pay off the credit card debt, which is at a high rate. This is a powerful financial concept you can use to leverage the cash flow of your current lifestyle for long-term personal benefit.

Of course, if you also apply the $5000 tax refund you receive (from example #1) to pay down your HELOC you will reduce the amount of interest that ultimately goes out on the HELOC and your Family Bank will be in a position to take on more new debt sooner.

One further benefit of this scenario is your credit score begins to go up. The credit rating agencies look at debt on a house differently than debt on a revolving credit card, so this shift can positively impact your credit score right away.

An Even More Beneficial Family Bank Example

As first, these simple examples may seem trivial, recapturing a couple of grand of interest over time. Let's assume that you just earned $40,000 profits on a flip investment property, which you desire to reinvest. You realize you will need to set aside about one-third of that for taxes, so you decide to put $25,000 into your Family Bank to capitalize it to be in the position to take on new debt.

Then you decide you want to buy a new car, on which you will need to finance $20,000. Of course, there is no issue getting qualified for this loan—you are the one who decides it's approved. Let's assume that you looked into financing it at the car dealership, and their proposed rate was going to be a 5 year loan at 7% interest or $396.02/month. That would be the same terms you would choose to pay your Family Bank. In this way, using your Family

Bank is not costing you any different than if you funded the purchase from your dealer, as you traditionally would have done.

Over the next 5 years, as you pay off this loan, you recapture the $20,000 principal and the $3,761 interest that would have gone to someone else. As you continue to cycle and recycle money through Family Bank loans, you are building an increased capital base on the principal and interest recaptured. Growth of these recaptured funds starts small but compounds over time as you increase the velocity of these funds.

Stacking Benefits With Your Family Bank

The long-term benefits of continuing to direct chunks of capital that come into your life into your Family Bank, and then lending it out for your credit oriented lifestyle needs is just a start. Think about the opportunity to stack benefits with a high return on an investment basis with a loan from your Family Bank.

Let's presume that you have a permanent life insurance policy that now has a cash value of **$250,000, and it is generating an annual return on that cash balance at 5% interest. You discover** that your local bank will lend using this life insurance policy as collateral at 3% interest, and you elect to start out with a $100,000 loan.

The important element is that *you can access liquidity based on the life insurance policy without it having to take a distribution, which would reduce the long-term compounding of your policy's cash value*. By collateralizing your policy, you are able to create powerful financial arbitrage with huge spreads, while at the same time the cash value of the insurance policy continues to compound. Some insurance policies allow you to borrow against cash value directly, but always check the rates with your local bank. Borrow

from whichever source creates the greatest spread with the lowest interest rate.

Let's assume that you put that $100,000 into nice, safe private loans, which generate 12% return. At this point, you have created an arbitrage spread of 9% (12%-3%) on $100,000. Your life insurance policy is safe and secure, as it always has been, whether you are leveraging it or not. Meanwhile, you have created $9,000 additional income from this incremental investment just utilizing the power of spreads. You have created a new investment opportunity out of thin air just by proactively utilizing the equity available to you.

In reality, during the same period of time, your life insurance policy has been earning 5% (within the policy) and 9% (using the policy as collateral to fund a private loan). So for the money you are redirecting, you are earning a combined 14%. **Stacking benefits can magnify returns in substantial ways.** By leveraging the equity that is already in your life, you have turbo-charged your financial growth plan. If you recall, from our discussion on the time it takes to double your capital when compounding, at 5% it will double in 14 years, while at 14% it will double in 5 years. Stacking benefits = reducing time.

Now picture what could happen as your life insurance policy cash value grows to $1,000,000 and more over the long-term. You could be generating huge income streams with very modest downside risk. All because you elected to have your money/equity working much harder.

If you decide to plow this extra income back into your Family Bank, you can accelerate the capitalization of your bank. More and more of your life expenses can be financed internally, rather than externally, and each additional loan recaptures more and more principal and interest. Once your Family Bank has significant

holdings, think about all of the things it could fund. It can make loans on cars, pay off current debts or pay college expenses. Money that used to go to 3rd parties is now retained and re-circulated for the family's benefit in perpetuity. It is all done with legal loans, but loans you completely control.

And as illustrated, once you eliminate high expense family debt and have further lending ability, have your family bank shift the strategy to lend on investment opportunities to stack the benefits and earn twice on the same money. It doesn't make sense to have your family bank pay off low interest rate debt like home mortgages when these funds can be directed toward private lending for greater spreads and benefits.

Such is the power of structuring your finances—leveraging the cash that flows through your life in multiple stacked benefits.

Insurance as a Perfect Wealth Building & Preservation Tool

Insurance has always been a focal point in many people's retirement plans, particularly when they reach the distribution phase in your final trimester. The goal during this time of life is to minimize all types of risk, so you are not stressed financially or unduly constrained in your lifestyle choices. Just like a farmer, planning ahead can strengthen the harvest and provide more bounty for you and your family.

There are many faces of risk that you should be attempting to reduce at this phase of life, including the risk of losing principle in stock bear market cycle swings, the risk of retirement account fees and taxes overburdening your investments ability to continue to

grow at rates higher than inflation and the longevity risk of outliving your retirement nest egg.

One way to do this, if your retirement savings are in Wall Street securities, is to *move capital out of the investment classes you designed for growth during the accumulation phase into a position where your principal is protected, and as you need income, it will be tax favored*. It means placing your capital in a position where the value will not be subject to risk in a bad economy. And putting yourself in a position where, should you pass away, your spouse or heirs won't have to deal with the headaches and expenses of probate.

Special types of insurance annuities can provide powerful financial benefits including safety of principal, potential growth that is greater than inflation, tax deferred accumulation and additional income throughout your retirement years. Because annuities are contracts which are backed with insurance, they are the only GUARANTEED performing asset in one's portfolio.

There is one provider in the Philadelphia market promoting this concept as: "Crash Proof Your Retirement Account".

While there are hundreds of unique annuities offered, there are two major classes of annuities in general: immediate annuities (move capital in as a lump sum and start collecting a guaranteed income immediately) or deferred annuities (make monthly / quarterly / annual premium payments and begin collecting a guaranteed income at some future point after your account balance has accumulated.) All of the annuities I'm discussing include an insurance death benefit.

Another differentiator is how the money compounds inside the annuity. This determines whether your return is fixed (like a CD with stated return) or adjustable (a popular version is an Indexed

Universal Life Annuity or also called a fixed indexed annuity which is tied to the stock market in a very unique way). Your capital actually isn't invested in the market, rather the insurance carrier ties to the performance of the market in sophisticated ways through options. In this way, when the market goes up, you can gain a portion of the growth in your account, but if the market declines you don't lose any of your principal balance. These are structured so you only participate in a portion of market growth. In that way the insurance company can earn its fees without charging your account. But unlike the broker with the mutual funds, there is no fee that hits your account balance should the market go down.

These specialized annuities are a way of using an insurance vehicle in a unique way. Traditionally, the way insurance policies are structured, the majority of your premium went to building up a huge death benefit. They weren't structured for benefit during your life. However, using the power of finance and tax benefitted environments, there are ways to structure the tool to minimize the death benefit and maximize accumulation of cash value, which can be accessed whenever you desire. When this is done, you *accentuate the benefits you can utilize as a financial leverage tool during your life*.

I like to consider insurance annuities as possibly becoming your own *private pension plan* once funded. One key benefit of a pension plan is that the other party is responsible for managing the investment and providing stated benefits for as long as you live. There is no chance you will outlive your nest egg if it has been transferred into an insurance annuity, which has an obligation to pay you a stated amount as long as you live. Of course, to receive a substantial monthly income, you need an annuity with a massive cash value.

To achieve a properly structured asset, you must find a life insurance specialist who focuses on this unique use of the tool. The characteristics to discuss with the agent includes if the annuity:

- Has an annual reset to the base value when your interest is credited, so the new balance becomes your new floor below which the principal balance is guaranteed
- That it is structured with reasonable caps/spreads or participation rates if it is tied to the market gains
- If it's an index tied to the market with a cap, you want month to month point crediting so you participate in the monthly swings of the market, not just an annual credit
- Is structured so you are able to withdraw a minimum of 10% of your value each year without any surrender fees (you may have needs to access your account liquidity)
- Provides provisions for long-term care; your access to account liquidity is enhanced should you or your spouse need to go to a nursing home
- Pays the full accumulated value as a death benefit

I perceive two different strategies for use of life insurance annuities as a wealth building and wealth preservation financial tool.

If you are young and healthy, setting up a deferred annuity early in life when you should be striving to save could be the perfect wealth builder. Because you are young and healthy, the whole program is based on low rates for the death benefit provision, and you have a very long-term for modest premiums to accumulate and compound. Set it up to make your payments for a specified time (perhaps 20 years), and then let the balance continue to grow and grow as compounding hits the key inflection point of the hockey stick. When you reach a later stage of life, rather than paying annual premiums, you are taking monthly distributions—tax free.

The income stream, once distribution begins, can be huge if it has decades to compound.

If, on the other hand, you are currently in a later segment of your life with limited retirement accumulation and need to build wealth quicker, I have covered several strategies of using privately structured investments to build rewards quicker with reasonable risk. Then, at some point, as you are nearing or into retirement, you may choose to transfer out of some assets that continue to have some risk and into an immediate insurance annuity that is risk-free and provides an income benefit for the remainder of your life.

A Tax Avoidance Strategy Few Are Aware Of

It should be obvious that the less the IRS grabs, the harder working your net after tax money can be. One of the key principles of Harder Working Money is that you should work to structure your financial foundation to be as tax efficient as possible, while you also work to maximize returns and minimize risk. This will maximize accumulation earlier in your buildup period, so you have more capital to compound. And it will maximize what can be distributed later in life, when both time and capital are so precious.

There is a tax favored way to access income in retirement that has been available for over the past 50 years that most financial planners don't take advantage of—simply because they are unaware or don't have one's financial assets appropriately structured. I'm talking about generating income from an insurance asset and the EXCLUSION RATIO. This can be an important tool because it is *a legal way to not report/not tax 85% of the income generated by this asset over a 10 year period!*

When you own certain insurance assets, there are tax loopholes related to specific annuities. There is a portion of your annuity

income that the IRS considers a return of your original principal, and this is not taxed. So you can turn on an income stream and keep it flowing for an entire decade, reducing your tax liability to only impacting 15% of the flow. And the longer you wait to turn on this benefit, the higher the tax savings can be.

This wealth preservation strategy must be planned for in advance; your assets must be properly structured, and to take advantage of it, you should choose an appropriate period of your life to exclude the taxes. But it can be a great tool in your Harder Working Money toolbox that knowledgeable advisors should help you take advantage of.

Chapter 8—SUMMARY INSIGHTS AND PRINCIPLES

By reading this book, I hope that your awareness is broadened and perhaps you begin to see possible new pathways to prosperity. I intended the messages throughout this book as a positive paradigm of possibilities that virtually any person can utilize to improve his or her financial position in the near term and work toward financial and time freedom in the long run. I am attempting to demonstrate to masses of people, who are not where they desire to be in funding their retirement, that there are proactive ways forward through the principles of Harder Working Money.

The primary strategy I advocate is focused on generating cash flow. When you master the techniques, you can create rushing rivers of passive income that more than cover the expenses in your desired lifestyle. This can free up your time to pursue your passions and serve others.

Most of what I've discussed regarding privately structured deals is creating cash flow from spreads on leveraged money…as George Antone taught me → *focus on the Financing Game.* Discover reliable and safe ways to create cash flow leveraging other people's money or skills or relationships. This is the quickest, most reliable path to prosperity for those willing to privately structure deals.

There is a fundamental difference between investing and financing. Financing is structuring a deal to shift risk and expense to others, as well as shifting the risk/reward paradigm in your favor. Investing is more about speculation that a desirable outcome will

occur. Do I do both? Yes, but I invest to generate more capital to be able to transition it into sustainable cash flow.

I believe when you fully understand leverage and efficiency principles, you will be able to maximize the utility of the cash that flows through your life, as well as build new passive income streams that can last into perpetuity. This is creating Harder Working Money.

How Do You Manage Money?

One of the key foundations we covered is how you choose to manage the money that flows through your life. I like to characterize people's choices as 3 types of financial patterns on earning, spending and saving:

- Credit Buyers—*spend before earning*, often live beyond their means because of available credit; however, must pay up interest to the lender which compromises their ability to save.
    - o Very risky approach because always paying more for everything purchased on credit—and must continue to earn more to afford debt payments plus maintain credit worthiness.
    - o Few credit oriented buyers will ever reach prosperity because it's not in their nature to save.
- Cash Buyers—*earn before spending*. This is a prudent approach of budgeting; however the hidden cost is the opportunity of what they could have been earning on their money if it was invested before spending, so they are giving up wealth building potential on the cash that flows through their life.

- o   Perceived to be safe, but is only focused on present needs, not particularly building wealth for the long-term.
- o   Once cash buyers build a savings regimen into their budgets, can follow a plan toward specific ends of building long-term prosperity.
- Wealth Builders—*invest in assets that earn before spending*, generate recurring streams of passive income which can fund lifestyle expenses, now and through retirement. When reinvesting earnings, they also generate compound returns, building up long-term equity.
  - o   The preferred strategy of the affluent to protect and grow generational wealth because the focus is on investing before spending.
  - o   Massive Wealth Builders also *employ special, little know strategies*:
    - ▪   Build up a storehouse of capital in a vehicle that benefits from guaranteed growth regardless of market cycles—tax free! (Permanent life insurance structured to maximize cash value accumulation.)
    - ▪   Borrow the money they need for significant lifestyle expenses (e.g., cars) or for additional investments from their own Family Bank (can be capitalized by cash value life insurance, leveraged equity, etc.).
    - ▪   Recapture the interest they would be paying anyway to other lenders by paying back the Family Bank loan with interest, then recycling these funds to pay off consumer debt or utilize funds on investments creating arbitrage spreads.

I am attempting to demonstrate how I'm utilizing the power of finance as a Wealth Builder to flow capital through assets that will add benefits to my financial plan, as well as fund my family's lifestyle with monthly income streams while my portfolio accumulates equity over the long run.

Offense & Defense

Just like in sports, there are two distinctively different sides in the game of finance and investing.

Most people focus on the *offensive game,* which is about chasing higher and higher returns or compounded gains in equity. My personal choice in offense is originating privately structured deals, focusing on inefficient markets (private lending, real estate, etc.) where returns are possible that can be several times the results the masses are achieving in their traditional stock and bond portfolios. But even if you choose traditional securities, there are proven better low fee performers like an index on the Standard & Poor 500, which allow you to participate in broad market upside without specific stock risk. This is a long term buy & hold strategy, not attempting to time the market. As we have discussed in the book, regardless of the performance yield, returns can become substantial over the long-term, once you are compounding interest on top of interest.

The core offensive concept of successful retirement planning is simple: growth your portfolio to the point at which the interest or cash flow from your investments will generate enough passive income to support your desired lifestyle without having to work.

The *defensive game* is about protecting the downside, conservatively managing your finances and structuring investments in ways that try to ensure return of capital, as well as return on

capital. It's about structuring your game for efficiency. Once again, I see advantage in privately structured deals where downside risk can be reduced or mitigated and the tables of risk/reward can be tilted in your favor.

Since it is less common for most people to consider the downside, let's summarize a few important principles covered in the book. There are *4 primary constraints on wealth building from a defensive perspective:*

Market cycles: Market sectors are always going through a bull or a bear phase and long-term buy and hold strategies ride the waves up and down. As we discussed, emotional buyers and sellers who attempt to time the market often have sub-optimal results, simply because of when they buy and sell. The primary issue with market cycle loss is it is totally out of your control. Some believe broad diversification of your portfolio is a prudent defensive strategy. I prefer the concepts of stabilized cash flow real estate, private lending and annuities, which have stated returns and experience less market fluctuation.

Taxes: can really crimp results of compounding your growth as we demonstrated. By building your retirement program in a tax deferred, or even better, tax-free environment, you can generate significantly better results. As well, certain incomes like from rental properties or business profits are incentivized and taxed at lower rates than earned income. I am of the opinion that taxes will likely go up for the most productive among us in the future. If you generate a substantial income, it would be good to be proactive in setting up your financial house to legally minimize your taxes, or you may discover that most of your efforts put little in your coffers at the end of the day.

Interest: "Compound interest is the 8th Wonder of the World! Those who understand it—earn it. Those who don't—pay it."

(Albert Einstein) While credit has become a part of most people's lives, defensive players realize that interest charges on routine life expenses can be debilitating to wealth building. Few people understand the true cost of what they are paying for things purchased on credit, including interest in the payoff. One simple example: you finance the purchase of a car at the dealership—$30,000 and you are happy they approved you for 7.5% interest on a five year loan. The $599/month payment fits in your budget. However, as you pay off the car over the next 5 years, your payments will total $36,068. In my book, that means you paid 20.2% more than the price of the car (this is due to the true cost of money at 7.5% when amortized over a 5 year period). Savvy defensive players set up their own Family Bank and begin to recapture this interest for their long-term benefit. Savvy defensive players also understand that paying interest on good debt for cash flow assets enables leverage to control more assets under management and earn more cash flow. They become experts at creating spreads. Remember to evaluate loan constants when you are dealing with paying interest to control your spreads.

Fees: If someone is providing a valuable service, they deserve to be compensated. However, realize that fees that hit your account every year on the total account balance have a huge impact on your results. Every 1% annual fee will end up shifting 20% of your long-term return to the house. Too many people's retirement accounts' growth is getting stunted by fees eating up the majority of their gains. I prefer privately structured deals where fees are minimal or completely non-existent for funding partners.

Defensive players should always *limit portion size participation* in specific asset allocations. I believe it is good practice to not have all of your eggs in one basket—unless the basket is a broad index of the market. If you desire to purchase a specific stock, and stocks make up 30% of your portfolio, and you limit any one stock to 5%

of your stocks, then the most you could lose with a complete crash of that stock is 1.5% of your portfolio value. Similarly, when I'm doing private lending, I don't want all of my money tied up in one loan. While I have faith that the deals I do are good deals, it is a more responsible position to have my private lending money spread across several loans.

Savvy defensive players **establish exit plans up front in a deal**; they know when they buy at what point they plan to sell, as well as what they expect to get out of the transaction. Even if you buy stocks with the intention of holding them long-term, if you always place trailing stop orders, you will never lose more than a chosen percentage of your peak performance price if the asset has an unexpected setback, and you won't end up owning a turkey that you wish you had exited. Whether it is in stocks or in assets like rental properties, it's important to understand how the exit is an important part of the transaction and should be planned for from the beginning.

When I finally had to go through my dad's portfolio of his stocks in his estate, I noticed that he had purchased many small company stocks that perhaps he had heard about in investment newsletters over the years. Apparently, my dad was a buyer but never a seller. Probably close to one-third of the stocks in his portfolio were junk. Maybe these companies had performed for a time, but several had been languishing for years, and a few had even gone out of business. I'm sure he didn't know. But that's the point, isn't it?

Defensive players **consider inflation effects and the projected value of their dollars over time** when evaluating their long-term financial plan. Securities must grow more than the value of the dollar declines just to stay even. This is the reason traditionally "safe" securities like treasury bonds or CD's are loser bets in today's economy. However, businesses and hard assets like real estate with utility value tend to have pricing that reflect monetary

devaluation and inflation, so these assets can protect buying power. And if you have long-term debt like a mortgage on a rental property, you will eventually be paying it off with cheaper dollars. Some experts recommend adding precious metals to your portfolio to be a hedge, performing like an insurance policy. While they don't provide cash flow, if the dollar crashes, gold may have significant offsetting gains.

Defensive players realize that *every dollar you control can either make you interest* (have it work for you to earn more through a financing opportunity) or you can *place it in a speculative investment* (hope that it compounds and builds equity through appreciation over time), or you can *spend it and give up the opportunity of having it provide any return to you over the long run*.

Efficient Versus Inefficient Markets

I attempted to clearly explain the difference in opportunity between the orderly efficient markets where it is tough for the little guy to win, and inefficient markets where intellectual capital and relationship capital can trump financial capital for the benefit of the small investor.

- When a market is efficient, it is easily systematized and attracts big money
  - o $ flows in and out easily (liquid)
  - o Units are fungible/comparable (easily replaced by another of like kind)
  - o Attainable on a national scale, opportunities are universal
  - o Risk/reward easily assigned and comprehended— generally symmetrical so it caps the upside of what

can be earned unless one is willing to accept significant risk

- o Example: stock & bond markets
- When a market is inefficient, it is comprised by discrete transactions that tend to have unique attributes
  - o Units are dissimilar and must be individually evaluated/valued
  - o Relationships and local knowledge are critical to discovering extraordinary deals
  - o Risk/reward not easily assigned and deal specific— can be structured for asymmetrical advantage, which provides opportunities for big returns without sizable risk
  - o Example: real estate, private lending, private placements

I trust that you now comprehend the special opportunities and advantages available in inefficient markets, if you can personally learn to spot them/structure them or join into deals with other people who can and are seeking partners.

Everyone Needs a Plan

I am confident that, at this point, you realize it's up to you to create a retirement funding plan that matches your life phase, education and financial requirements to sustain the lifestyle of your desires. People must decide if their primary focus will be focusing on capital gains (building equity) or cash flow (building income) and whether they will be a more active or more passive investor. For the reasons outlined in this book, I have chosen cash flow because it is what pays for living expenses and I believe will be a quicker, more direct path to financial freedom. I am currently in an active

role and look forward to becoming more passive as I reach my financial freedom point.

The following are the asset classes I'm currently focused on:

- Private lending for higher yielding cash flow as a conservative foundation of my plan. I like that, in lending, most of the risk is shifted to the borrower, and it generates a relatively secure and predictable income. I also appreciate that, since the loans I'm doing are all short-term and spread across several deals, these funds are moderately liquid. When you have a broad portfolio of short term loans, one is always close to coming due.
- Cash flow rental properties for tax sheltered cash flow and equity building will be my long-term workhorse. I like that the real estate sector is not highly correlated to financial markets and tends to be less volatile. I appreciate that properly purchased rental real estate maintains stable values during time of turmoil—regardless of cyclical ups and downs in the residential real estate market, if a cash flow property is not over-leveraged it comes down to just maintaining the income flow regardless. I also appreciate that RE can be acquired with leverage that my tenants will pay off in the long run. In this way, it creates both income and equity. And I love the tax benefits of owning real estate to shelter income. Of course, at this point, I own both single family, as well as small to medium size multi-family rentals, and I intend to own more multi-family in the future.
- I have formed a business with a contractor doing residential flips as a safer way to generate substantial cash influx. In the short-term I view this as a way to earn an income to live on, while I build my multiple cash flow streams in lending and cash flow properties. In the longer run, this may

continue to be a way to generate capital I can transition into cash flow assets.

- I am currently evaluating when, and if, annuities will fit into my longer-term plans. If I were 20 years younger and in better health, their inclusion would be a no brainer. However, since in most of the most attractive of these assets you must have your capital sit ideally five to seven years and accumulate a strong cash value before you can touch it, I'm concerned about directing too much of my capital at this point into lower earning vehicles, while I'm still in an aggressive accumulation phase. As well, since these assets are insurance based and my health and age suggest higher cost premiums/lower returns—this asset isn't perfect for my personal situation. But I do clearly comprehend the several benefits of this sector in eliminating risk, having liquidity and tax advantages. I recommend everyone evaluate how an Index Universal Life annuity could fit into their financial plans.

I've also recently set up the Leigeber Private bank—to recapture interest on debts we need to pay down and become my temporary storehouse of liquid funds awaiting reapplication.

Opportunities for Partnering and Learning From Others

I have frequently heard it said that your net worth will gravitate toward that of the 5 people you are around most. This is because our thoughts and activities are heavily influenced by our close associates. I can certainly state, since I've left the world of corporate marketing behind, the people in my inner circle have changed as I became an entrepreneur. I have proactively sought out people who have the same level of drive and worldview that I

have. I believe it is prudent to take the road already traveled by someone who has done it before and helped others pursue the same vision. In this way, my path has been clear, and I have confidence I will prevail.

I have formed strong bonds with mentors who have enlightened me, as well as with partners who I own properties and businesses with or am lending with. Deal sharing or just mastermind associations have frequently created synergy because we all perceive things differently, and hearing other's perspectives can help you better understand the reality we face. As well, I choose to invest with people who earn their living on investments, who are participating in the same deals—not listening to a salesman who is living off of commissions selling whatever his company tells him to sell. I see great benefit in clear alignment of interests.

Roy Williams of the Wizard Academy (a small business marketing educator) has a great quote: "A smart man makes a mistake, learns from it and never makes the same mistake again. However, the wise man finds a smart man and learns from him how to avoid the mistake altogether." I hope that I am in the process of becoming a wise man and that you have benefitted by learning of my experiences.

Foundational Principles of Harder Working Money

Here are 8 foundational principles of Harder Working Money that I believe all can benefit from:

1. We each must accept the fact that *we are solely and completely responsible for our current financial situation* and the choices we make

    a. If we are to achieve and sustain prosperity, it will be because we pursue the education and action plans to fulfill a specific plan to achieve it.

    b. It's more important to know what we desire and why than how we are going to get it, that emerges along the way.

2. Money alone doesn't make us richer or poorer (everyone has millions of dollars that that flows through their lives in a lifetime)—it's ***our education on how to best utilize what flows through our lives*** (money and opportunities) and ***the relationships we foster*** that we must leverage to create wealth.

    a. The journey to making /creating one million dollars of equity happens $100 at a time—don't expect overnight success, rather compound successful moments.

    b. With an income oriented retirement plan, we are able to drive more income from our wealth than our work and this approach is sustainable through the retirement phase.

3. ***We must earn more than we are taxed and spend*** to build wealth.

    a. Earnings accrue from our labor, business systems we control and the power of our capital to earn returns.

    b. We must develop routine saving and investing plans and treat these accounts as sanctuaries, never to be plundered for short-term enjoyment.

    c. Legal savings in taxes or reductions in fees are just as beneficial as increases in earnings for wealth building.

    d. If we constantly live in a mental frame of instant gratification, we will never be prepared to fund our lifestyle requirements during retirement.

4. ***Risk vs. Reward***—while most mass market investments are symmetrically priced (reward is consistently priced with risk taken) → ***smart money seeks an asymmetrical relationship*** (big upside potential with little downside exposure).

    a. We are more likely to find asymmetrical rewards in privately structured deals and inefficient markets (real estate, private lending, private placements).

5. People either ***invest for cash flow or capital gains***.

    a. Most people focus on building equity through Wall Street securities they hope will produce capital gains.

    b. We prefer to focus on cash flow because this is what pays for living expenses and is a more direct route to financial freedom.

        i. Generating cash flow comes down to generating arbitrage spreads, which can more quickly be accomplished using leverage (other people's money).

        ii. ***Leverage can replace time in the journey to financial freedom*** (leverage money, knowledge, people).

6. ***Creating multiple passive income streams is the key to wealth***, not big wins on an equity play.

    a. Devote more time to wealth building activities—there are many opportunities available, but you must reach out and find them.

    b. The more our income > expenses, the more we can invest in new income streams.

    c. Seek to develop profitable wealth pairs, where the income generated exceeds the cost of capital to buy the asset

    d. There is significant leverage when our investments are creating enough profits to buy other

investments...this can create rushing rivers of cash flow like a mountain stream after a heavy rainstorm

7. *Planning our exit*
    a. If we are currently employed in the rat race, we should simultaneously develop Plan B, generating multiple streams of passive income, so at the timing of our choice, we are financially prepared to walk away from our traditional source of income.

8. With proper planning and investing in private deals, we *can control the financial environment in which we operate*, rather than being a slave to a dysfunctional economy which may wreak havoc in the financial markets.
    a. Our own economy > National economy. When we create a vibrant personal economy, we are less at risk of the financial markets' volatility

It's time to decide if you will commit to a new plan of action directed at funding your retirement through an income oriented approach:

Desire → Knowledge → Purposeful Action → Persistence → Life Altering Results

I thank you for taking the time to ponder my concept of Harder Working Money. I wish you well on your journey to achieving monetary and time freedom.

May the Force of Harder Working Money Always Be With You ☺

More information is always available at
www.HarderWorkingMoney.com

I'd love to understand more about your journey and see how we can help each other achieve the financial and time freedom we all desire. Who knows, perhaps we'll even find the opportunity to do business together at some time as well.

I can always be reached at 214-682-0164 or
Jay@HarderWorkingMoney.com

Bonus Offer

If the Harder Working Money concepts have struck a chord with you and you would like to delve deeper into how the partnering approach can work for you on a passive investor basis, I would like to offer you free wealth creation strategy session valued at over $250. This conversation will be directly with Jay Leigeber, the author of Harder Working Money.

For this to be a value to both of us there is a simple questionnaire that I request you to fill out prior to our conversation. This wealth builder strategy conversation will last up to one hour. We'll cover where you currently are in your retirement plan, what type of investments you have had success or failure with in the past and how a change in your strategy may be beneficial. We'll begin to see if there is a fit between the passive income opportunities we regularly share with the people we have come to know and your financial needs/expectations.

This would just be the beginning of a relationship. There is no pitching of current opportunities. For SEC compliance reasons we'd just be starting down a path of getting to know each other and sharing concepts of what may be possible down the road. There is certainly no obligation when you commit to spending the time and personal information.

Should you be in the greater Philadelphia area perhaps we'll get together…that is certainly the best way to get to know each other. If not, we'll do the strategy session via phone or Skype if that works better for you.

Please go to www.HarderWorkingMoney.com/FreeStrategySession and provide your contact information. You will receive a simple questionnaire by return email. Once the questionnaire filled out and returned we

will coordinate a mutually agreeable time our session. Our time is limited for these free sessions because we choose to spend the majority of our time ensuring we deliver the best results for our passive investor partners.

Thank you for considering this opportunity to get to know each other. Avoid disappointment and future regret—sign up for your free strategy session today!